MYSTICISM IN JAVA

IDEOLOGY IN INDONESIA

Other Niels Mulder titles published by The Pepin Press:

Inside Indonesian Society
Cultural Change in Java

Inside Thai Society
Interpretations of Everyday Life

Inside Southeast Asia
Religion • Everyday Life • Cultural Change

Niels Mulder

MYSTICISM IN JAVA
IDEOLOGY IN INDONESIA

THE PEPIN PRESS
AMSTERDAM AND SINGAPORE

First published by The Pepin Press in 1998

© The Pepin Press BV

ISBN 90 5496 047 7

A CIP record for this edition is available from the publisher and from the Royal Dutch Library, The Hague.

This book is edited, designed and produced by The Pepin Press
Copy-editor: Rodney Bolt

The Pepin Press
POB 10349
1001 EH Amsterdam
FAX 31 20 4201152
Email: pepin@pepinpress.com

Printed in Singapore

Contents

Preface

At the end of April 1969, I finally reached Yogyakarta. It had been a long, at times arduous, trip on my little motorcycle — a Honda 65 — from Bangkok. I had flown to that city from the United States where, at that time, I was an assistant professor at Northern Illinois University. This American connection had everything to do with my earlier — and first serious — research in Thailand. In that country, I had met Ladd Thomas, coordinator of Southeast Asian studies at 'Northern'. When I returned home to the Netherlands in 1966, he had been quick to encourage me to join his group of Southeast Asia specialists at DeKalb.

The fact that I had ever gone to Thailand in the first place was no coincidence either. It had much to do with Indonesia and the spectacularly blundered Dutch decolonization. In 1958, I had wanted to visit this country of my dreams, but relations between Jakarta and The Hague had by then deteriorated to the point that Hollanders were being expelled rather than welcomed. Passing by, I stared at Sumatra's coast line, and visited Malaysia instead. When I graduated, Indonesia was still off-limits, and so Professor C.C. Berg, with whom I read Bahasa Indonesia, advised me to go to Thailand, which he described as another Indianized state in Southeast Asia, about which, as he put it, 'we have no knowledge at all here'.

I was in Bangkok during the momentous events of 1965–66, but as long as I remained preoccupied with Buddhism and Thai, Indonesia was really beyond my horizon. Yet, after I had made it to N.I.U., my desire to go to Java was rekindled, and I started working on a research outline to go there. I saved up money and, in January 1969, I obtained 'leave of absence without pay', and was on my way. To get as much mileage out of my investment as I could, I travelled via San Francisco, Hawaii, Japan, the Philippines, and Bangkok. There I bought my little Honda and, six weeks later — through Thai dust, over Malaysian asphalt, then through the mud of Sumatra, and across the potholes of Java — I made it to Central Java's 'cultural city'.

As forbidding as the Indonesians had been under the old dispensation, so welcoming were they to visitors under the new regime. I had arrived in the country with a Thai bike and on a tourist visa. In Pekan Baru, I had been given an 'explanatory letter' to clarify why I rode a foreign vehicle; at LIPI, the Indonesian Academy of Sciences, I had been processed within two days. My visa had been converted; I could do research; had police clearance; and was allowed to stay on for two years. The New Order was still very new, and all bureaucratic hurdles had been cleared with youthful speed. This is the truth, however incredible it may sound these days.

Now, I have been coming to Yogyakarta for almost thirty years. Somehow, I have become part of the furniture. I know many people there, and many people know me. This makes life easy, whether for research or just socially. In my type of work, it is not really possible to separate the two. In Yogya, among the members of its middle classes, I am in the part of Java I am fascinated with, and that I explore; everything I hear and experience there contributes to what I think to know about the place. Every visit is a new adventure and, as a good traveller, I share my tales with audiences and readers. Hence this book.

Introduction

It was quite accidental that I stumbled on Javanese mysticism. I simply appeared to be asking the wrong question. It went like this. I was interested in the political aggregates that — in the literature — had been described as *aliran*. So it came naturally to me to use that word when explaining what I hoped to do in Java. And since the people I met were helpful, they suggested that I listen to certain persons whom they held to be very knowledgeable about aliran. Eagerly, I made contact with these individuals, and in no time at all I became involved in the fascinating world of mysticism.

In those days in Yogyakarta, the word aliran was not associated so much with national politics, as with mystical groups which cultivated *kebatinan*, that is, 'the science of inner man'. There were many streams of interpretation, and differences in practice. The word aliran means stream: hence, stream of thought and, by extension, the group of people adhering to a certain stream of thought. In this way, the *aliran kebatinan* with which I became involved were nothing more, or less, than sects that held certain ideas about what is often referred to as Javanese mysticism.

To westerners, mysticism has, possibly, an aura of secretivity. It is seen as a very personal affair. It touches on private convictions and religiosity, and thus is seen as a private matter. This means that it is not easily brought out into the open, and that to start probing into it is generally held to be impolite. It is not for public consumption. In Java, I soon found out that matters of religious insight are very much in the open, and can easily be discussed. Many people are even eager to state or exchange their views, not with the purpose of 'converting' their audience, of winning them over, but just to talk about things that preoccupy them, that they find eminently interesting.

Many Javanese appear to be in love with their own civilization, and they certainly like to talk about many of its aspects. The more so, perhaps, with an interested foreigner. To many of them, kebatinan, or the inner dimensions of life, are most attractive: often they see these as the very heart of their culture. Things are not what they appear to be, but have a hidden core that fascinates them. They are adept at discussing the symbolic meaning of the shadow theatre based on the *Mahabharata* mythology. They speculate about hidden forces — whether spirits, or secretive political manipulation. In the same vein, the esoteric science of inner man is not so private after all. This is not to say that everybody is knowledgeable or talking about these things, but many people are. They are fond of explaining the symbolism of the ritual meal, of religious practice, of chance occurrences, of chronograms, and suchlike. In brief, the symbolic — and the mystical — dimensions of life constitute an important field of interest.

Thus, taken almost unawares, I became involved in a captivating and enchanting world of mystical practice, magical manipulation, secretive interpretation, outright nonsense, and deep meaning. Soon I forgot my original, respectably sociological, intentions. I went on into culture, into Javanese fields of knowledge, into patterns of thought. How do these people conceive of the world, of their lives, of their relations? How do they explain them? The fact that their reasoning might be at odds with practice, or with the hard facts of life, I took in my stride. I became interested in culture per se, not as an explain-all, but as an interesting social product. Culture arises as a fruit of human association, which it may temporarily spellbind, but human society is not the captive of culture, or patterns of thought for that matter.

Over the years, I have steadily published my Javanese findings. The original idea for this book was to collect my writings on mysticism and patterns of thought. This idea was fostered by the constant interest in my dissertation — now long out of print — and the relevance of Central-Javanese culture to the understanding of New Order Indonesia. President Soeharto's regime is given to projecting itself as a cultural order, justified in the name of 'tradition' and 'authenticity'. Its programme to build a Pancasila state peopled by Complete Indonesian Men is cultural indeed — and heavy is the investment in values education. To understand what is going on, we need to comprehend the Javanese background of thinking about all this, and so the purpose of this book became to juxtapose Javanese mystical patterns of thought with those that seem to inform the cultural engineering of nation building in Indonesia.

It is of utmost interest to compare these two patterns of thought, and to trace the parallels they evince. Doing so, however, inevitably raises historical-sociological questions. Where do these Javanese patterns of thought hail from? What is the historical constellation in which they arose? Why did people cling to them, especially in the period running up to 1975? And are they still relevant to the highly changed circumstances since then? Obviously, the Indonesian government thinks so, and continues, indefatigably, to work on the brains of its subjects. But isn't it so that these people live in a world increasingly remote from the ideal of the Pancasila state?

These are the main questions pondered in this study. In doing so, the book first explains the resurgence of Javanism, as exemplified by the postwar efflorescence of kebatinan mysticism. This cultural revival is the subject of the first chapter. Upon this, the assumptions of mystical, or Javanist, thinking will be analysed in the second chapter. The resulting paradigm is illustrated by the characteristic example of lottery prediction. Following upon this funny and amazing little excursion, we are taken back to the practice of mysticism proper. In the third chapter, several types of adepts and adherents are distinguished, such as the lonely virtuosi, the guru who basks in the limelight, and the crowd of people attracted to the mystical experience. To all this belongs an ethic, and even a social philosophy, that should be understood in terms of a prevailing view of social life; it is the subject matter of the fourth chapter. The fifth then expands on the type of society in which the mystical practice arose and made sense.

In the sixth chapter, the most salient points of the Javanist world view have been arranged in a logical fashion — meaning that they are mutually connected and reinforce each other. The pattern of thinking becomes clear. Although this exercise entails some repetition, it is useful in bringing focus to the following chapters. Of these, the seventh draws attention to the current resurgence of Javanism. This revival has little to do with mysticism, or the practice of kebatinan, as such, and all the more with politics and the position of the Javanese as the majority population of Indonesia. The Javanese, and thus Javanization, are spreading everywhere. They educate all and sundry on how to be Indonesian. This indoctrination programme is part of all schooling, and the chapter takes its inspiration from the contents of the national curriculum. In its last section, the parallels between Javanist ethics and patterns of thought are considered, which brings to light a cardinal point of divergence: whereas mysticism has the potential of setting free, Pancasila propaganda aims at capturing the individual, at ensnaring him as a subject of the state.

In chapter eight, we review whether there is any fit between what is propagated, and how life is lived. It will appear that the state ideology has been inspired by idealization of village life, also known as Asian Values; it has thus precariously little relevance to modern urbanity in a globalizing setting. It propagates a 'collectivism' that never was, and that is very much at odds with praxis, and with the images evoked by Javanese-authored fiction. In conclusion, therefore, it is safe to state that the moral education programme does not agree well with modern life and, more seriously, that it does not prepare people to constructively and responsibly engage themselves in it. In parallel to mysticism, it may, at best, stimulate persons to keep their distance, and to keep themselves to themselves. This is amply illustrated by our second excursion into fiction.

The book closes with a summary of patterns of thought such as they surface in the practical conduct of life. These concern, among others, the self-presentation of the ruler; the importance of obligation and gratitude; basic religiosity; academic discussions, and the treatment of prisoners. All this is followed by a bibliographic note that should make good for the paucity of footnotes and immediate references. A list of selected literature also compensates this conscious omission. Indexes complement the book, including a glossary of repeatedly used Javanese and Indonesian words.

CHAPTER 1

Resurgence of Javanism: kebatinan mysticism

Cultural revival

The Javanese constitute the single biggest ethnic group in Southeast Asia. They comprise some forty-five per cent of the two-hundred-million-strong population of Indonesia. As with most Indonesians — well over eighty-five per cent — they adhere to Islam. Yet, as may be expected, such massive religious adherence is culturally diverse, not only because of the considerable diversity of the Indonesian population, but also because of subcultural variation among the Javanese themselves. As of old, they recognize two broad streams of religious commitment: those who pray, and those who do not. 'To pray' means to perform the five obligatory ritual prayers every day. People who do so are known as *putiban*, that is, white or pure ones who take their religious duties seriously. Nowadays, these people are often referred to as *santri*. They contrast with *abangan* ('red ones') that is, the mass of nonreligious people, or those who do not observe the perfunctory Islamic rituals.

Under the heading 'Ideological Conflict', a current sociology text for the superior grade of high school explains the distinction as follows:

> There are differences between the universalism and expectations for the afterlife of santri, and the pragmatism and relativism of abangan in Java. Abangan see Islam as the religion of the Arabs, and that is why they are not living up to it wholeheartedly. To them, it is not so important to always praise God as to behave in a good and honest manner. They downgrade the importance of ritual behaviour because they hold that real purity is a matter of a person's inner life; it is a matter of the batin. This is why the place of prayer is not in mosque or church, but in the upright heart. In contrast to these opinions, the santri accuse the abangan of being heretical, of adhering to a mistaken interpretation of Islam, of being polytheists, and suchlike (Tim 1996:43).

These differences in the valuation of religious practice have been part of life in Java ever since the advent of Islam. At that time, religious life was inspired by basic animistic thinking and so-called Hindu-Buddhist doctrines and practices that, combined, offered a fertile matrix for magic, mysticism, the veneration of powerful souls, spirit cults, and the worship of holy places. All this was not in marked contrast to the mystical and devotional type of Islam that reached the island. As a result, and probably also because of Muslim egalitarianism, the religion of the Prophet was able to establish itself rapidly in the coastal areas of the island. Further into the interior, the older form of society — aristocratic and hierarchical — was able to maintain itself, while at the same time incorporating forms of Islam. Over time this gave birth to a South-Central Javanese civilization, centring in the royal courts of Surakarta and Yogyakarta, that is generically known as *kejawèn*.

The common dictionary gloss for kejawèn, or *kejawaan* in Indonesian, is 'Javaneseness', and 'Javanism'. This last word is a descriptive label for those elements of Javanese culture that are considered to be essentially Javanese and that define it as a unique category. These elements are generally thought to hark back to the Hindu-Buddhist period of Javanese history, and combine in a philosophy — in the sense of a particular system of principles for the conduct of life. As a system of thought, Javanism is singularly elaborate, containing a cosmology, a mythology, a set of essentially mystical conceptions, and suchlike. These give rise to a particular Javanese anthropology: a system of ideas about the nature of man and society that, in its turn, informs ethics, customs and style. In short, Javanism provides a general universe of meaning; it is an integrated body of knowledge that serves to interpret life as it is and as it appears to be.

The Javanist tradition is extremely rich and draws on a vast literature that spans at least a thousand years, from the oldest, highly Sanskritized sources to historical and legendary accounts of the old kingdoms, such as the *Pararaton* and *Nagarakertagama*; from the history of Mataram, as recorded in the *Babad Tanah Jawi*, through innumerable mystical and religious treatises in which the influence of Islam becomes gradually more apparent, to the encyclopedic *Serat Centhini* and other nineteenth-century works by court poets; from Mangkunegara IV's influential didactical poem *Wédhatama*, through the works of twentieth century thinkers, such as Ki Hadjar Dewantara and Ki Ageng Soerjomentaram, to the writings of contemporary novelists. In other words, it is a continuous tradition that is fully alive, often exemplified by present-day secular and mystical literature and, for the adepts, by the interpretation of the widely popular shadow theatre plays that have Javanized *Mahabharata* mythology as their subject. This Javanism also pervades the current explanations of the Pancasila state ideology, and the ideas underlying the creation of the Complete Indonesian Man.

In a half-conscious half-unconscious way this Javanist tradition serves as a referent to explain practical behaviour, at least for those who find their origin in South-Central Java. Of course, these people may also refer to more recent universes of meaning — such as being Indonesian, or adherents of a particular political theory, or members of a particular religion. But as soon as they refer to life close to home, to family relationships, the conduct of everday life, the nature of understanding and knowledge, the relationship between self and society, and even the meaning of being Indonesian, they tend to implicitly or explicitly refer to kejawèn categories of thought that demonstrate their Javaneseness and their belonging to a generic Javanese culture.

Javanism, or kejawèn is not a religious category, but refers to an ethic and a style of life that is inspired by Javanist thinking. So, while some people may express their Javaneseness in religious practice, such as, for instance, in mysticism, it is in essence a characteristic culturally induced attitude toward life that transcends religious diversity. In Yogya, I met many Javanese who take their Islamic duties seriously and who qualify as santri on all counts. Yet, they were also Javanese discussing life in the perspectives of *wayang* (shadow play) mythology, or interpreting the five daily prayers as a personal encounter with God; many of them appreciating the ritual meal (*slametan*; see below), as an important mechanism of social integration, or having a remarkable sense of obligation to visit their parents' graves. Moreover, in ethical terms, they would measure themselves as seriously as any Javanese in being *ikhlas*, that is, sincere in purpose. This corresponds to the Javanese notion of being *sepi ing pamrih*, that is, not being guided by egoistic motives; placing the interest of others before personal interests.

Although there is no doubt that ideas about kejawèn may be best expressed by those who are most deeply educated in the secrets of

Javanese culture, and that this Javaneseness is most often best represented by the old court and government-oriented elite and its descendants — the so-called *priyayi* — it should be made clear that consciousness of their own culture is a widespread phenomenon among the
Javanese. This cultural awareness often serves as a source of pride and
identity. It is those people who cultivate their Javanese cultural heritage
in depth who may be considered as kejawèn. In the words of an informant: 'They are the people who know and who can express it; they are
the one's who have "concern" and who know that all has a meaning,
and is significant to the understanding of one's personal life'.

Be this as it may, kejawèn as we know it today is clearly a product
of the meeting of Islam with older Javanese civilization; of the domesti-
cation, or pacification, of Javanese royalty by the United East-Indies
Company (VOC); of the colonial encounter of Javanese and Dutch. These
very conjunctures compelled the Javanese to reflect upon their own
being and, what's more, stimulated the construction of a Javanese identity. Such reflection and construction are the result of the confrontation
with otherness, and so, over time, even oppositions could develop, such
as santri-abangan; Java versus Europe; an orientalized East against a
materialistic West. Such oppositions exacerbate differences, caricature
them and, yet, often play the part of self-fulfilling prophecies: people
start believing them, and shape their behaviour accordingly.

Such changes in identification and consciousness develop gradually. Sometimes, though, they experience an upsurge. Intensified contact
with the Middle East stimulated Islamic consciousness in Southeast Asia,
and the religious modernism of Mohammad Abduh in Egypt inspired
Muslim reformism in Java. The latter took shape in the Muhammadiyah
organization of 1912, which from then on aspires to fuse modernity and
religion. With the founding of the Sarekat Islam in the same year, Islam
also became an anticolonial and anti-Chinese symbol. The essential
modernity of these organizations naturally drove the more traditional or
Java-oriented majority of santri to unite, too. And thus, in 1926, the
Nahdlatul Ulama association was established to maintain the authority
of the ulema, sufist mysticism, and the veneration of the saints — all of
which is anathema to the modernists.

Predictably, changing times, the gradual introduction of public
education, and the global circulation of novel ideas, also fostered

kejawèn thought. Interest in mystical theories and practice was strongly promoted through contacts with western theosophy. Javanist cultural awareness and native education were promoted by the Budi Utomo association of 1908 and the Taman Siswa school movement of 1922, and were in part a reaction to European schooling. With so many modern organizations and such a ferment of ideas, there is little cause for wonder that the 1920s witnessed the flowering of Indonesian nationalism too. It is not apposite here to retrace the efflorescence of new ideas and consciousness in the early part of the twentieth century. For our purposes, we should note the cultural resurgence then going on among modern and tradition-oriented Muslims, among mystics and kejawèn devotees, among secular and religious nationalists, and among an assortment of incipient political parties.

In this book, we shall concentrate on the kejawèn cultural revitalization in the post-Independence period. Such revivals occur in periods of rapid change, similar to the one outlined above, when answers are sought to basic questions affecting peoples' identity and consciousness. Consequently, many Indonesians sought for answers in their respective backgrounds, be they modern Islam, traditionalist practice, secular modernism, or Javanist thought and mystical practice. The latter two form a particular focus of this study because of their topical relevance to understanding the current teaching of the Indonesian state ideology and the special position of kejawèn culture among the country's political elite.

The rise of Javanese mysticism

As we have noted, intensified contacts with the wider world resulted in the cultural-cum-religious movements that together became known as the National Awakening. While this surge in all sorts of consciousness was subsequently emasculated by the colonial regime, the advent of the Second World War again kindled the flames of nationalism, and of Islam. Whereas the Dutch government had always been suspicious of Islam, the Japanese recognized and invested in its anticolonial and nationalistic potential. Therefore, during the deliberations about the shape of independence, Muslims advanced the idea that Indonesia be established as an Islamic state. To them, this meant a country founded on belief in The One God, in which the adherents of Islam would be obliged to live according to the laws of their religion. This last stipulation became known as the Jakarta Charter. To the majority of the secular, often Javanist-oriented, nationalists on the Preparatory Committee for Indonesian Independence, the clause was unacceptable, and it was thus not written into the Constitution. The Constitution guarantees 'each citizen the freedom to choose his own religion and to worship according to his own religion and faith'. Thus, belief in The One God, or monotheism, became a principle of the Indonesian state as a matter of course, while any sort of compulsion of how this was to be carried out was rejected. Although this was not to the satisfaction of certain Muslims, the extremely heterogeneous nature of the Indonesian population necessitated the building of the new state under the motto 'Unity in Diversity'. This nationalist idea carried the day, and was further enshrined in the Five Principles, or the Pancasila, that formulated the unitary basis of Indonesian nationhood: (1) the belief in one God Almighty; (2) humanity that is just and civilized; (3) the unity of Indonesia; (4) democracy guided by the wisdom of representative deliberation; and (5) social justice for all.

The war, the physical struggle for independence, the terror within the Revolution, and the insecurities of how to give shape to a democratic Indonesia, resulted in those unsettled conditions that always prove to be a fertile ground for political polarization, religious zealotry, soul searching, and doubt about identity. They gave rise to what became known as *aliran* politics. Aliran are, literally, streams — in this case of political commitment, which divided the population into the camps of nationalists, communists, traditional and 'modern' Islamists. In the long period running up to the first national elections in 1955, these mutually antagonistic groupings organized themselves from the national level down into the small towns and villages, where they established a plethora of associations of all sorts, each of which identified with one of the four main political parties. In their competition, tolerance gave way to strife. The Javanists among the nationalists became more conscious of their syncretistic kejawèn identity, as opposed to orthodox Islam. The abangan mass — often associated with the communists — became more aware of their class position vis-à-vis the landownership of righteous santri. But 'modern' and traditional Muslims, too, had their squabbles. Apart from fostering an unruly political climate almost opposed to Unity in Diversity, these separated stands reinforced cultural identifications, such as kejawèn. For many, this was expressed in Javanese mysticism, also known as *kebatinan*.

In 1952–54, when Clifford Geertz did his field research in Paré, he described the practice of mysticism as a priyayi, or high class, phenomenon. He also noted the attraction mysticism exercised on the abangan mass. Some of the mystical groups he described had 'a large abangan admixture', but these groups were 'based on the teachings of high priyayi gurus in the court centers and ... modelled after the more elevated sects' (1960:309). At the same time, however, he observed the emergence of a 'modern abangan cult', Permai, that was both a political party and a mystical association (112).

According to Geertz, Permai represented an attempt to lend contemporary relevance to traditional abangan beliefs, on the one hand relying on esoterism and healing techniques, and on the other being a 'vigorously anti-Islamic social organization composed mainly of town laborers, employed and unemployed, impoverished rural radicals, and estate workers past and present' (113). The membership held Permai to be 'pure native science' — characteristically revealed in meditation — based on 'original', that is, pre-Islamic and even pre-Hindu beliefs, which combined the nationalist Pancasila ideology with old Javanese religious patterns (115). In this way, Permai appeared as an adjustment to a changing social context: 'It is a religious system designed for a peasant come to town' (118).

Geertz's discussion of the Permai cult brought to light the strong opposition to Islam of certain abangan groups. During the 1950s and 1960s, this hostility would gradually increase to the point of confrontation. He further recognized that the effort to organize mysticism in sects was a new phenomenon. These post-war sects struck him by their 'almost denominational form', which he interpreted as a reaction against the congregational organization of the practising Muslims. Moreover, the various sects in Paré were beginning to form a loosely organized group, vaguely tied to similar associations in other towns. The mystical leaders appeared to realize themselves that they would have to organize in order that their request that the Ministry of Religion accord them the recognition and status of the 'official' religions, such as Islam and Christianity, be effective (349). These various observations about an emerging trend appeared to have come true less than two decades later.

The expansion of mystical movements during the early fifties drew the attention of Javanese mystics themselves, and of the Ministry of Religion. By 1951, the mystic-cum-politician Wongsonegoro was already active in bringing together the various schools of Javanist thought in a Committee on Philosophy and Mysticism. He had also founded a political organization, the Great-Indonesia Party, which aspired to assemble the various mystical sects under his leadership.

In 1952, the Muslim-dominated Ministry of Religion advanced a narrow definition of religion. To qualify for recognition, a religion should have a prophet and a holy book; besides, it should enjoy international recognition. This 'definition' would exclude mysticism as a valid religious expression because, to the mystic, 'God'[1] is revealed directly to the heart, and not through intermediaries or sacred texts. Because of the opposition of the Balinese Hindus, the definition had to be withdrawn. In the years to follow, the Ministry noted a steady increase in the number of 'new religions' and mystical groups. As a result, it established *Pakem* (Body for the Surveillance of Faiths) to supervise them, in 1954. The idea of such an authority was nothing new: the former colonial government had also kept close watch on folk-religious movements and their charismatic leadership, which could arouse the peasantry into violent protest. In hands of the Ministry of Religion, Pakem became the watchdog against utterly anti-Islamic spiritual movements.

The year 1955 was important in clarifying the cleavage between Islam and Javanese syncretism. The result of the first general elections showed that Indonesia did not politically identify as a Muslim country. Nationally, the Islamic parties polled only 42 per cent of the vote, while sympathies in Java were even more unfavourable: Central Java voted 30.3 per cent Islam, and the Yogyakarta area — where the research was done — only 24.5 per cent. Obviously, there was little sympathy for the idea of becoming an Islamic state. In the same year, the *BKKI* (Congress

1 'God' refers to the 'immanent' Javanese conception of God. Without quotation marks, the word God refers to the more 'transcendental' ideas of the Middle-Eastern monotheistic religions.

of Indonesian Mystics) was established under the leadership of Wongsonegoro, and it convened its first conference in Semarang. The following year, the BKKI held its second congress in Solo (Surakarta); it declared that kebatinan mysticism was not a new religion but rather fostered the quality of religious life in general. This second congress was attended by two thousand representatives of an estimated two million people throughout Indonesia.

Clearly, Javanese mysticism had a broad popular base; it had also spread beyond the island. In 1957, the President was asked to recognize kebatinan as being on the same level as the organized, official religions, and to see to it that mysticism be represented in parliament. In 1958, however, President Sukarno warned the third BKKI congress of the dangers of *klenik* (black-magical) expressions of mysticism. At that, the congress reiterated that kebatinan was no 'black magic', but supernatural power and 'white magic'. Meanwhile, the outcome of the regional elections indicated an overall decline in identification with politicized Islam: in Central Java, the Muslim parties still polled 29.2 per cent of the vote; in the Yogyakarta area, only 22.6 per cent.

In 1960, a unique congress convened in Pekalongan, at which representatives of the Indic-Javanese mystical tradition and Muslim sufi mysticism met and deliberated to find their common ground. At a youth conference, the Minister of Education, Professor Priyono, proposed that 'synthesism' and 'syncretism' be recognized as the essence of Indonesian culture, and that belief movements should be legally protected. Meanwhile, the fourth congress of the BKKI in Malang resolved that there were no essential differences between religion and mysticism: religion emphasized ritual, while mysticism stressed inner experience and the perfection of man. At the instigation of the prime minister, Pakem was taken over from the Ministry of Religion by the Ministry of Justice, which meant a decrease in the former's authority.

In 1961, the Minister of Religion again proposed a definition of religion, with the purpose of denying mysticism its place under the Indonesian sun. Religion should be characterized by a holy scripture, a prophet, the absolute lordship of The One God, and a system of law for its followers. Meanwhile, the police had taken over the supervision of mystical groups in order to prevent social unrest. The following years were characterized by a rapid expansion of mystical movements.

21

Communist infiltration in many of them became apparent. To bring order to the emerging religious anarchy, President Sukarno decreed that only Islam, Catholicism, Protestantism, Hinduism, Buddhism, and Confucianism enjoyed official recognition; groups threatening these established religions, or the stability of society, would be prohibited and dissolved at the recommendation of the Minister of Religion, the Public Prosecutor, or the Minister of Interior.

In the aftermath of the coup events of September-October 1965, Muslim youth groups, with the backing of the army, moved to eradicate atheistic communism from Indonesia, resulting in the terrible slaughter of an estimated half a million abangan citizens. To some Muslims, it appeared that victory was near. The new dispensation declared that henceforward people must recognize themselves as followers of an established religion — which was to be marked on one's identity card. In other words, not to have a religion was no longer legal, and to save one's neck, it was politic to look for protection by affiliating with any of the six recognized religions. Islamic *da'wah* (missionary efforts) in the villages were intensified, and everywhere civil servants, students, and other citizens had to attend courses aiming to develop a religious mentality. Meanwhile, the police and Pakem dissolved those mystical groups that were suspected of being infiltrated by the Communist Party.

The slaughter of suspected 'communist' abangan in 1965–66, and the pressure to show that one had become an obedient Muslim, boomeranged on Islam. In their quest for protection, many nominal Muslims opted to seek membership of the Protestant and Catholic churches; in Java, their membership increased very rapidly in the two to three years following the coup, and churches had to cope with the problems of 'massive baptism', shortage of infrastructure, and insufficient personnel, to deal with the flood of 'converts'.

Of similar interest is the emergence of Hinduism and Buddhism in the years since 1967. Both these religions had experienced the beginnings of a revival during the fifties and early sixties. They regard themselves as the living embodiment of the religion and culture of the glorious days of Majapahit, before the advent of Islam and the humiliating days of colonization. Their rapid growth during the late sixties, from virtual obscurity to the several hundred thousand registered members of today, indicates a growing cultural-historical consciousness and, especially after the outburst of 1965–66, a refusal to regard themselves even formally as Muslims of the statistical category. They point to the Borobudur, the greatest single Buddhist monument on earth, or to the many exquisite Hindu temples that can be found all over the island; they fondly relate the Sabdopalon prophecy, in which it was foretold that Javanese Hindu-Buddhist culture would revive five hundred years after the defeat of Majapahit at the hands of Islam (sometime between the 1470s and 1530s). Apart from this historical justification, Javanese Hindu, Buddhist, and mystical thinking is nourished by *Mahabharata* mythology ('the bible of Java'), which relates the times when ancestors and gods were still on earth and instituted the great rules of life and tradition.

Politically, mysticism appeared to advance steadily with the majority of the army and administrative leadership firmly rooted in a kejawèn background. Soon after the military's rise to power, it proved to be as suspicious of politicized Islam as the preceding Sukarno government. In the running-up period to the 1971 general elections, the regime had persistently outmanoeuvred both the Islamic parties and the remnants of the Partai Nasional Indonesia *(PNI)*. Meanwhile, the position of mysticism as a valid form of religious expression was strengthened. In 1970, under the aegis of the government party Golkar, a body was organized to attempt to unify mysticism in a broad single movement, eventually striving for legal recognition. This Badan Kongres Kepercayaan Kejiwaan Kerohanian Kebatinan Indonesia *(BK5I)* held its first congress at Gadjah Mada University in Yogyakarta, again under the titular leadership of Wongsonegoro. Later, in December of the same year, mysticism was formally incorporated into Golkar when the organization established a coordinating body of spiritual and mystical leaders. Within Golkar, this body is juxtaposed with similar coordinating entities, such as that of the Muslim ulemas *(MUI)*. From 1971 onward, it became known as the Sekretariat Kerjasama antar Kepercayaan (*SKK*, Coordinating Secretariat of Faiths).

Here, it is important to draw attention to the shift in vocabulary. Up into the sixties, the word kebatinan equated with Javanist mysticism. Yet, not everybody appeared to be happy to be regarded as such. According to certain modern mystical movements, such as Pangestu, the kejawèn mystical tradition entailed much more than training the *batin* (inner core of man) to meet with its divine origin. Kebatinan also allowed for contacts with the spirit world, magic, and polytheism, and modern-minded adepts did not feel comfortable with that old-fashioned heritage. To distinguish themselves, they preferred words derived from the ideas *jiwa* (soul) and *roh* (spirit). In this way, kebatinan, as 'science of the inner man', became juxtaposed with 'science of the soul' and 'spirituality'. All were subsumed under *kepercayaan* (faith). From the late fifties, when the President warned against black-magical, klenik expressions of Javanist mysticism, and on into the seventies, we may note a growing emphasis on monotheistic mysticism — on the striving after contact with The One God. At the same time, mystical foremen interpreted the constitutional position of faith to equate with *agama* (religion), and to avoid misunderstanding, the word kepercayaan has since been used to refer to the successor movements of kejawèn mysticism.

The idea that there is a constitutional basis for the mystical heritage was reinforced by the clauses about religious development in the programmatic Outlines of the Course of the Nation *(GBHN)* formulated by Parliament in 1973. These clearly set religious life and life based on faith side by side as equal partners 'to serve God in accordance with the Pancasila and to together develop society'.

This policy was supported by the then non-partisan Minister of Religion, Mukti Ali (1972–78). In his view, there was no harm in giving some form of official recognition to Javanese mysticism. On the contrary, in allowing it to surface as an acknowledged practice, that may even present itself along with the official religions on a weekly hour of state television, it could be domesticated by depriving it — to some extent — of its attractive aura of esoterism and secretiveness. On the other side, the Minister argued, Islam should not build its position through apologetics and in opposition to others, but generate strength from within through better and more enlightened education, and the development of self-confidence.

This sympathetic treatment of faith is about the closest Javanese mysticism and belief systems have got to recognition by the Ministry of Religion. Somehow, its officials did not know what to do about Javanist beliefs, and there was no support to give them space by conceding a directorate-general on equal footing with and next to the existing ones for the established religions. In 1978, the knotty issue was cut. Faiths were allotted a bureau, the Direktorat Kepercayaan kepada Tuhan Yang Mahaesa — Bureau for Faith in The One God — under the division of culture in the Ministry of Education and Culture. Faiths became culture rather than recognized religion. Be this as it may, Javanist religious life kept its forum on television, and incidentally replaced Confucianism in the religious representations in the 'Beautiful Indonesia' in Miniature Theme Park. While the high-handed New Order reduction of Chinese ancestral expressions to Buddhism says something about the position of the Chinese in Indonesia, it also vacated the lot that was reserved for Chinese religion when the park was under construction. As a result, and gloriously juxtaposed to representative buildings of the five remaining religions, we now find the complex — in 'Javanese' style — devoted to Faiths, called Sasana Adiroso 'Pangeran Sambernyowo', in English referred to as the Discussion Hall for Indonesian Beliefs.

Thus, while not quite recognized as religion, by the end of the seventies Javanese mysticism appeared to be firmly institutionalized. From then onwards, enthusiasm for this expression of Javaneseness seems to have levelled out, to be carried on by the more solidly established mystical associations, such as the sophisticated Pangestu and Sumarah movements, the internationally known Subud sect, and the more middlebrow Sapta Darma. In the eighties, and up into the present, these, and other denominational forms of mysticism, hold their own in a society where Islam, as a timely identity option, is spreading and has come of age. Meanwhile, though, the confrontational aspect of the discourse between Islam and mysticism, characteristic of the fifties and sixties, has eased out at the same time that the practice of kebatinan has been moving into a modern, monotheistic direction. This is not to say that the kejawèn heritage is diminishing in importance. For the time being, at least, it is a pet child of the regime, which reinterprets this heritage in many ways in its desire to create a Pancasila state peopled by 'complete Indonesian human beings' who, incidentally, seems to hail from a mystified, generic South-Central Java.

The revitalization of kejawèn

The phenomenal rise of Javanese mysticism in the years since independence cannot be explained by any single simple reason. Most apologists of the official Middle-Eastern religions in Indonesia emphasize that the rapid growth of the number of mystical groups indicates dissatisfaction with established religion. In their view, the popularity of mysticism can, to a large extent, be explained as a reaction to the dogmatism and ritualism of institutional religion that neglects the need for mystical expression and inner experience. If the monotheistic religions were better equipped to cater to these needs, the Javanese would readily fill the mosques and churches; mystical sects would simply become superfluous.

In my opinion, this explanation misses the point. These apologists see all Javanese as Muslims, or potential Christians, who can be brought into the fold, while they fail to see that, in the eyes of kejawèn adepts, they themselves are newcomers who are felt to be foreign to Java. Implicitly, these representatives of monotheism think that the advent of modernity and the loss of certain time-honoured forms entail the need to embrace a 'modern' religion. As a result, they failed to recognize the attraction of kejawèn culture, and its genius in finding own ways to adapt to the modern world and social change.

To many Javanese, it is disappointing that the mystical fruit of their soil is not recognized as a fully respectable expression of devotion equal to the imported faiths. Whereas they will seldom find fault with the diverse doctrines, they may find certain expressions of religious behaviour thoroughly distasteful. To them, 'God' is in the heart, and life should be a continuous prayer to the Almighty. They do not see why one should pray to God five times a day, or in a church, or why such prayers must be blared from loudspeakers on tops of mosques. In kejawèn thinking, God is not an unapproachable, distant judge; on the contrary, 'God' is closer to man than anything else. They recognize the ritual expressions of all religions as useful, as elementary steps on one's way to 'God', but while Islamic and even Christian ideas have influenced Javanese mystical thinking and terminology, they can neither accept Mohammed as the last prophet nor Christ as the unique saviour. Because of their intimacy with ultimate reality, they recognize that revelations may descend every day. Yet, their mystical message does not so much promise salvation or heaven, as it is directed towards interpreting worldly existence in a cosmological perspective.

A second widespread interpretation views the rise of mysticism as a reaction against the onslaught of modernity and related moral decadence. According to the historian Sartono Kartodirdjo, unsettled conditions may cause, much like the former colonial domination, 'a persistent sense of dysfunction' and 'a sense of cultural deprivation' (1973:5); these cause religiously inspired movements to arise. The anthropologist Koentjaraningrat interprets the practice of mysticism primarily as a withdrawal from the difficulties of everyday life into a world of dreams and inner experiences, and a yearning for the past. Subagyo seems to agree with this argument, and adds that 'all mysticism develops as a sign of protest and criticism against present times' (1973:126). And certain psychiatrists see membership of mystical groups primarily as a search for individual equilibrium and fulfilment of dependency needs — something especially popular in times of social stress and turmoil.

This second type of explanation holds better than the first. Javanese mysticism does not fail to provide meaning for suffering, and the unruly and alienating present affirms the wisdom that is contained in mysticism and its practice. The everyday experience of powerlessness seems to confirm the wisdom that it is better not to hope for anything, to be content with little, to make a virtue out of suffering, and to turn inward rather than to look for rewards in the outer world. With the present development towards and experience of anonymity and insignificance in wider society, all sorts of religious expression appear to thrive, from fundamentalism to new sects and cults, from holier-than-thou moralism to individual-centred mysticism. In brief, there is no shortage of options to search for identity, equilibrium, and esoteric company.

Thus, whereas there is truth in the escape-and-compensation interpretations of the scholars we referred to, and while there is an element of withdrawal in mystical practice, the phenomenon of organized mysticism as such seems to indicate a movement of people who attempt to find truth and identity in their own cultural heritage. They actively deal with changing times, and try to find their own solutions. They are not busy escaping from anything. Besides, the practice of mysticism is not restricted to the poor and the powerless, but is also highly popular among intellectual members of the middle classes, the military and certain elite groups. These facts — that mysticism is both an elite and an organized phenomenon, and that it is society-wide — suggest that the revival and vitality of kebatinan mysticism in the immediate post-independence period can best be seen as a search for cultural expression and identity in a time of transition and change.

CHAPTER 2

Basic premises

In Javanese mythology, derived from the Indian epics of *Ramayana* and *Mahabharata*, life is seen as a battle between anarchy and order. In the *Mahabharata* cycle, disorder is represented by the Kurawa faction; they symbolize arrogance and self-glorification; lust, passion, and desire; egotism and vanity. They are the ones who are out of step with the will of the gods, and who do not respect the great order. When they are in the ascendency, life in the cosmos and on earth is characterized by disorder, uncertainty, and injustice. The Kurawa are opposed by the Pendawa, the five brothers who stand for piety, selflessness, and trust in the righteousness and necessity of divinely ordained order. When they prevail, the cosmos and life on earth will enjoy quiet, harmonious, just, and prosperous conditions. In the Bharata Yuddha, that is, the great war, the Pendawa overcome the Kurawa, and order can be restored.

To the Javanese mystic, this model of the *jagat gedhé* (macrocosm) stands as a paradigm for man, as a *jagat cilik* (microcosm). Peoples' potential for anarchy is apparent in their drives and emotions, their passions and desires. It is these that tie them to the *lair* (phenomenal) world. Their *batin* (inner) aspect relates them to their origin, to ultimate meaning and moral order. In the mystical endeavour, people strive to subject their outer being to their inner potential; they hope to free their inner selves in a quest for reunification with their origin, and to experience the oneness of being.

Order is the condition that should prevail. Order means harmony with the cosmic purpose, and in its deepest sense, it means unity, the oneness of the all, of creator and created, of servant and master, of *sangkan-paran* (origin-and-destination). To Javanese mystics, life on earth is part of this all-pervading unity of existence. In this unity, all phenomena have their place and stand in complementary relationships to each other; they are part of one great design. This design is thought to constitute a regulated order where events do not happen haphazardly, or because of chance, but because of necessity. Somehow the outcome of history and events has been foreordained; it reveals itself because of the *ukum pinesthi* (law of necessity).

The unity of existence finds its epitome in its all-encompassing centre, in *Sang Hyang* (The One), *Hyang Suksma* (The All-Soul), that is, *Urip* (Life), from which all existence emanates and to which it has to return. It is Life itself that animates the order of cosmos and earth, that constitutes its essence and secret. This order is hierarchical, running from the grossest to the more refined manifestations of existence that are closer to the latter's essence and truth. In that hierarchy humans find themselves somewhere in the middle, tied, as they are, to the phenomenal world, and to the secretive essence of Life. Harmony with this ultimate principle of existence is the moral task of all that exists, and the noble purpose of the practice of mysticism.

At the ultimate point of the mystical journey, the world becomes inconsequential, but since the mystical pursuit results in the accumulation of great moral power, an advanced mystic will still shine like a beacon in the world, to the moral and material benefit of society. The practice of mysticism is, therefore, thought to foster the right life on earth, to bring about desirable conditions.

In former times, this idea of the benefit of mysticism for the world was highly institutionalized in the view of kingship. Kings were thought to be among the most powerful mystical elements on earth, to be receptacles of cosmic potency. Their worldly power reflected their charisma, that is, their receiving of a supernatural mandate to rule, known as their *wahyu* (also, *wangsit*). Such wahyu was a clear sign of their association with and concentration of *kasektèn* (cosmic potency), which was thought to radiate as a beneficial magical force from their persons to the populace, ensuring the latter's prosperity.[2] Their palaces were constructed as model images of the cosmos, symbolizing their position in this world as centre of the universe. The names of two of the remaining sultans in Java, namely, Paku Buwono of Solo and Paku Alam of Yogya, which both translate as 'axis of the world', are reminiscent of this thinking.

2 This thinking is kept alive at school where the kingdoms of old are presented according to the self-eulogizing *prasasti* (commemorative-stone inscriptions) in which the religiosity of the ruler is combined with the prosperity of the realm. It is also always reiterated in the mandatory descriptions of the kingdoms of righteous rulers in the shadow play theatre.

From the above, it may be seen that a close relationship is thought to exist between cosmic and worldly conditions. Because of man's mystical potential, he can penetrate supernature, which has consequences for life on earth and in society. If men submit to 'God' and steadfastly practise mysticism, or faithfully fulfil their religious obligations for that matter, their harmony with higher existence will result in beneficial moral and material conditions in this world. Conversely, an orderly society with justice and prosperity indicates a harmonious relationship with supernature.

The human and the cosmic orders are coordinated, are part of a whole, and if they strive for unity and equilibrium, life will be quiet and good. Such periods are known as *zaman mas* (golden periods), when just kings reign and people share in general prosperity. Yet, if people, and especially the worldly powerful, are guided by their passions and egoism, they will cause anarchy and chaos, injustice and insecurity, poverty and hardships. Such periods are known as *zaman édan* (crazy times). Then people will be inclined to hope for the arrival of a *Ratu Adil* (Just King), who will re-establish harmony. Nowadays, such messianic hopes seem to be pinned on Semar, the guardian spirit of Java who, as retainer of the Pendawa, represents the common folks, and their suffering.

Although cosmic conditions may explain the current situation in the here-and-now, it is ultimately man himself who has the power to influence these by his spiritual and moral behaviour. Logically, this results in a rather anthropocentric view of world and cosmos. The *cakra manggilingan* (wheel of history) appears to be oscillating between periods of mystical and religious enthusiasm and its ensuing prosperity, and periods of moral decay and unsettled conditions. Similarly, the *cakravartin* (wheel-turning king) does not so much project the cosmic conditions on earth as his own mystical-religious behaviour: if he is a wise king, a real *pandita ratu*, his realm will enjoy peace, justice, and prosperity — it will be like an ordered and quiet microcosmos that reflects its unity and harmony with divinely ordained necessity; if he is a weak or power-hungry king, the unsettled conditions of his realm will reflect his lack of wahyu.

Whichever way things are viewed and rationalized, it is clear that worldly and cosmic conditions arise because of coordination. Events are caused by their coordinated structure: a palace reflecting the order of the cosmos becomes an exemplary centre radiating divine blessing to kingdom and populace; it must bring about a just and prosperous society. Similarly, a king guarding his wahyu by way of mystical concentration must bring about improved conditions in his worldly power. Likewise, this is so for the personal mystical endeavour in which the outward, lair aspects should be conditioned by the inner batin. Spirituality, and the inner relationships that momentarily prevail between cosmos and society, explain — and cause — the current human condition.

The implied ideas of unity and interpenetration are reflected in the idea of 'God'. To mystics everywhere, the divine essence pervades manifest and secretive nature. 'God' is immanent in creation, is part of everything that is. In this understanding, the divine is indwelling in the inner core of man; it is the essence of his batin that, mystically, should be trained and developed to permeate existence. In brief, man partakes in the divine essence, he carries it in his innermost being, and to be serious about life means to develop it. Yet, this immanent potential is both elusive and real, such as when people say: '"God", I do not know; when I open my mouth and say "God", "God" is, but when I keep my mouth shut and do not utter this name, "God" simply is not there'.

When I submitted this thinking to a friend who is deeply interested in kejawèn culture, he observed: 'Does "God" exist? *Ana tan ana* (is, is not) is the way we express it. As long as we can think and use our common sense, "God" is not, but when we stop thinking, when we are anxious, dying, or at the end of our wits, "God" is. After all, from where do we come, where do we go? We must have an origin, a purpose, a direction. Our sangkan-paran (origin-and-destination), that is "God"; it is the force of life that is all around us. Whether we believe in "God" or not, we are part of it. Ki Hadjar called it *Kodrat alam* (the principle of Necessity) that conditions our existence. Yet he also taught us that we should strive to better ourselves, actively developing *budaya* (thought and culture). During the deliberations about the principle of "God" in our Pancasila, he was willing to concede that the principle of Necessity could be called *Ketuhanan* (The Divine), but he opposed the addition of *Yang Mahaesa* (The Only One), because in his view people should and can develop themselves by their own efforts. Or look at the teachings of Ki Ageng Soerjomentaram, for that matter. Right now his ideas are quite popular again. In his teachings of *Kawruh Beja (Science of Happiness)* there is no reference to the idea of "God" at all. For him, it is people themselves who can achieve *kasampurnan* (perfection) by developing their self-knowledge and their understanding of the nature of life'.

While Ki Hadjar Dewantara's and Ki Ageng Soerjomentaram's positions and influential teachings emphasize self-knowledge and reflection upon experience as the sources of wisdom, my friend — and most ordinary people — express the less self-confident position that each life is under the influence of a vague yet pervading divine principle that may be conceived of as origin-and-destination, or simply Life itself. To them 'God' is in the heart, it is the 'God' they feel; it is Life and their being part of it, or, in the words of a mystic, 'It is in every beat of my heart that I feel "God". It is Life that surrounds me and me being part of Life. It is within me and outside me. It is being born, being married and dying. What is, is Life, continuity of existence, our sojourn here being a mere stop on the road "where we pause to have a drink". Life flows and we flow with it, our task being to seek the continuance of that flow. We live from origin to destination. We come, form, and disappear; we go nowhere but fulfil the scheme of Life'.

Nowadays, this principle of Life may be rendered as *Ketuhanan Yang Mahaesa*, which is understood to be the divine principle that encompasses all. A word like Ketuhanan is essentially vague and full of mystery, referring to The numinous rather than to a personalized God *(Tuhan; Allah)*. The divine can be felt in the inner being; it is an experience of and personal encounter with essence and truth. It is not a confrontation with something that is outside the self, but the affirmation that one participates in the unity of existence.

This pantheistic view results in what may be called the 'cult of life'. It is the realization of the ultimate principle, of Life within the self. If that is accomplished, one 'has returned home'. There is thus little cause for wonder that the Javanist perspective downgrades expectations about the afterlife. Life must be accomplished in the here-and-now; it is a task to be fulfilled. People who have not completed their journey, may somehow be reborn to finish their duty. At its simplest level this may involve the idea that to accomplish life's course means to serve its continuity, that is to procreate, to have offspring. It also entails that morally defective people, criminals and misfits, may have to make good before they can fade from the face of the earth. Of people who meet a violent death, it may be thought that they were stopped in their tracks. They need to be reborn in order to complete their walk on earth. But then, expectations entail no more — and no less — than reunification. This was explained to me by the simile of a white sheet of paper. 'See, this is the All. Its whiteness is and pervades totality. It is both empty and everything'. Then my interlocutor drew, in pencil, a little circle somewhere on the sheet. 'See, now there is a body. Its inner core is still white; it is its origin, and its destination. But it is hindered from uniting with origin-and-destination by that manifest body. The mystic tries to overcome this barrier; death obliterates it'. Subsequently, he erased the little circle. The totality of the white sheet remained: everything and empty.

Such is the nature of Truth. The essence and working of reality, of the All, is not material (as the Latin-derived word reality suggests) but process and stream, as in the Germanic *Wirklichkeit*. Reality is its own cause and effect. It encompasses and is the void. It is *kasunyatan*. This Sanskrit-derived notion is normally glossed as 'highest wisdom' and 'truth in the religious sense'. In the Buddhist discourse, it derives from *sunya*, zero, O, centre, meaning void, and the all-comprising circle that symbolizes emptiness and concentrated essence. In life, one should strive to realize this insight; one's life is, belongs to Life.

The Javanese road to insight into reality is the trained and sensitive *rasa* (intuitive inner feeling). In mysticism, the essence of reality is grasped by the rasa and revealed in the quiet batin. By overcoming the fetters of everyday existence and the phenomenal world, man may free himself to really understand and achieve direct knowledge of the mystery of existence.

The order of life and cosmos is seen as a spiritual hierarchy that runs from the lowliest animals and material conditions, through the social hierarchy, into the realm of invisible forces, and up to the highest truth and cosmic essence. The worldly powerful and nobility are literally seen to be closer to truth, and thus in a more favourable position to communicate with higher forces, than the lowly man who depends on his relationship with the earth for his living.

However this may be, most palace-oriented mystical teachings also stress respect for the hierarchical order of the state as the first step on one's way to 'God': 'If one honours one's elder brother, one's parents, one's guru, and one's king, one thus honours "God"'. This emphasis on the hierarchical aspect of the social order is much less developed in mystical teachings circulating among common people. They may even see mysticism as a way to bypass the social hierarchy. This is not to say that they must not respect their social order — they must respect elders and teachers, and guard the harmony of living in their communities.

People are morally and mystically unequal. This is because some are entirely worldly, attached to matter and the emotional conditions of life, while others strive for the development of their spiritual powers. Besides, hierarchy is demonstrated by unequal capacities and unequal birth. Finally, every individual has to climb the spiritual ladder by himself if he wants to achieve true insight.

The notion of the essential oneness of existence carries over into the material world. Objects are possessed by the spirituality of their owner or maker, and may contain a power of their own. Natural happenings — be they droughts, volcanic eruptions, or plagues — have supernatural significance and stand as signs for the workings of the cosmos. Almost every Javanese household possesses holy heirlooms, generically known as *pusaka*, that should be revered and ritually respected. These objects possess sacred power that can be used for protective, magical, and mystical purposes. Similarly, the graves of ancestors, kings, reputed Islamic and mystical teachers are thought to be *kramatan* (holy places), which serve as sites for meditation in order to acquire insight and spiritual powers. The relationship between nature and supernature is so intimate that it is impossible to draw a line. Both participate in the oneness of existence, and ordinary objects may contain signs that are revealing of the cosmic process.

The licence plate of a general, the dress of a guru, the date of a ceremony, all may emanate omens that are relevant for future action. Similarly, signs and manifestations that come one's way through chance are rather understood to be co-incidences that reveal the cosmic coordinates of current conditions and events to come. The cosmos — including life, things, and events on earth — is a coordinated and ranked whole, a oneness of existence in which every phenomenon, material or spiritual, has a significance far beyond its face value. Mystically, however-er, the world and its tangible manifestations are of little interest. Man's sojourn on earth is seen to be a rather unimportant stop along the road where he 'pauses to have a drink' while on his way to reunification with his origin.

In summary, we can state that man actively and inevitably partici-pates in the all-encompassing unity of material and spiritual existence. The spiritual aspect is superior, more true as it were. In its highest qual-ity, it constitutes the origin and destination of humankind. Harmony and unity with ultimate essence is the purpose of all life. Potentially, man can participate in supernature in all its aspects, with the representatives of anarchy as well as with those of order. It all depends on how he attunes his spiritual behaviour. Nature and supernature mutually influ-ence each other, and causality is implied in their coordination. When coordination occurs or is brought about, events and conditions have to follow. This thinking is valid both for pure mysticism and for magic. It is nicely illustrated by the practice of prediction.

Lottery prediction

When I did my first research in Yogyakarta, people were under the spell of the *Nalo* (national lottery). A full ticket consisted of six or seven digits, and could be bought officially, but gambling on the tail, that is, the last two digits of the outcome, was far more popular. The streets were lined with the small stands of *bandar* (underground-lottery bankers), who sold the numbers 00 to 99. They paid seventy times the stake if the outcome of the tail of the national lottery coincided with the number bought. Basically, this was good business, but the risks were considerable. The main danger was arrest by police or the army, whose actions were entirely unpredictable. Generally, the authorities tolerated this form of gambling, but sometimes, towards the end of the week, they suddenly had an urge to maintain law and order, and arrested bandar almost at random. By that time, the bandar had collected a considerable amount of money, so that their seizure meant a good income for the servants of the law. Other bandar let themselves be detained on Thursday, and shared their income with the police while being unable to reimburse potential winners on Sunday because they had been 'arrested'. The *buntut Nalo* (gambling on the tail) was big business for the authorities, bandar, the people, and lottery outcome predictors.

I witnessed how Pak Amat became one of the most prominent lottery predictors in Central Java. He was of Christian origin, a graduate of Gadjah Mada University, an important man in his neighbourhood, the leader of a small kebatinan group, and an amateur student of Javanese psychology. He began forecasting the lottery, because members of his kebatinan group were insisting that he tell them, while he himself thought that his contact with supernature was sure and pure enough to warrant a try in that direction. It was a matter of controversy among kebatinan leaders in Yogya whether they should provide their followers with numbers, but Pak Amat began to foretell the lottery anyway. His first predictions were 'sure' numbers, which meant that if he said the outcome would be 15, he meant 15 indeed. At that time, his forecasts were based on simple symbols that he received as *ilham*, or inspiration, during meditation. His following, consisting of a few Javanese families and Chinese shopkeepers, lost some money but the matter was not taken too seriously; it was fun — partly serious, partly playful. On a certain day, however, Pak Amat received a symbol about which he was particularly sure. It looked like this:

With the participation of his following, he interpreted the symbol to mean 15 or 34. Fifteen, because the symbol could be read as 2+1+2=5, with 1 in the central axis, and 34, because 2-1+2 makes 3, and 4 was considered to be strong because of the two 2s. Everybody was pretty convinced by these interpretations, and all concerned played for very high stakes — the Chinese gambling as much as 100,000 rupiah (then US$240) on each of the numbers, the Javanese much less, but still more than they could afford to lose. The outcome was 95, and this spelled a crisis. Somebody in one of the Javanese families was ill, and there was no money left to buy medicine. Pak Amat felt miserable. The only solution was to re-establish order and unity by conducting a slametan (religious meal) in the house of the family that had been most hurt by the gambling. The ritual feast was to begin at 9 p.m. Everybody was present with the exception of Pak Amat. It was the week before the first Apollo mission to the moon, and all were talking about its possible success or failure, while evaluating its significance for the outcome of the lottery.[3] At that time, I ventured a tongue-in-cheek prediction on the outcome of next week's lottery by an esoteric interpretation of the word Apollo. Later, I was shocked to find that a few of those present had in fact bought the number I predicted.

3 In the late sixties, the venture of 'flying to the moon' was not the matter of course it may be today. In religious circles, such an endeavour could even be interpreted as blasphemy, as an insult to God's order. As a result, a certain Muslim teacher attracted attention when he declared such a mission not only to be haughty, but definitely impossible. Confronted with overwhelming evidence, he had to retreat from his position — and did it well: 'What does it really mean, some Americans flying to the moon? They can never match the Prophet: He flew straight to heaven!'

Pak Amat arrived around eleven, and played it masterfully. Apollo was forgotten and we began the slametan proper. During his prayer and his speech, he became very emotional. He confessed to be a sinner, a conceited creature of God, who had had the vanity of interpreting His will by giving sure predictions, without realizing himself that his inspiration only consisted of signs and hints. He repented, he wept, condemned himself for his vanity, and then, at the end of almost an hour, he admonished his flock, in a sublime counterclimax, that they should not doubt the authenticity of his inspiration. On the contrary, his symbol contained the truth and if people still doubted, they should turn the symbol against the light where, in mirror-writing, they could read 95 indeed:

Everybody present, including myself, was shaken and deeply impressed. It was clear that Pak Amat did receive very superior inspiration. Obviously, he had access to high knowledge that was hidden from his followers. As the story spread, his following grew by leaps and bounds. Although he still tried to satisfy his visitors with kebatinan speeches, it became increasingly clear that the people who gathered around him were primarily interested in his ability to predict the lottery. As a result, a few of his more serious Javanese followers became dissatisfied and dropped out.

Within a few weeks, Pak Amat became the most influential lottery predictor in Yogya. Hundreds of people visited him every day and at all hours, some coming from places as far away as Semarang or Solo. These visitors appeared to constitute a cross-section of the slightly more well-to-do urban population, representatives of all walks of life, from small traders in the market to Chinese shopkeepers, teachers, civil servants, students and graduates, soldiers and officers, male and female, young and old — and virtually all of them literate.

With so many people to interpret his symbols, signs and hints, there were always winners who gave credit to Pak Amat for their lucky number. His fame thus continued to spread, and soon he had to regulate the flow of visitors. On Wednesdays and Thursdays, he would speak to the crowds that gathered in his yard, and reveal the inspired signals containing clues for the draw on Saturday night. The following Sunday, he would interpret Saturday's outcome on the basis of his fore-telling. At that time, he also began to distribute stencils that contained a drawing, a cluster of ciphers, a text from the bible, and the hour at which all of these had been received in meditation. The people, howev-er, were primarily interested in his speeches, from which they took notes, and which some even recorded on tapes.

Pak Amat used these speeches to tell his audience about kebati-nan, about right and wrong, and often that Jesus saves if the sinner repents. He was fun to listen to; speaking in an odd mixture of Javanese, Indonesian, and Dutch, he easily drew the laughter of his audience. Being the son of a Protestant minister, he performed as a full-blooded preacher. He involved his congregation by asking questions, getting answers and by drawing spontaneous reactions.

Pak Amat enjoyed all this very much. He reasoned that his lottery predictions gave him the opportunity to redeem people by way of moral lectures — much like his father had done in church. He felt that the lot-tery might relieve the poverty of his public, and that he was doing good work because the government had organized the lottery to obtain funds for national development. Whatever his personal justifications and defence against the severe criticism from the church and the majority of kebatinan leaders in Yogya, people gathered around him to get some clue about the next week's draw. Obviously, they were not interested in the other aspects of his message.

These people were particularly keen to observe Pak Amat's behav-iour. As a guru, he was thought to have access to high knowledge and insight, and to be so much in step with supernature that his actions were coordinated with higher truth, and could thus reveal the future. This idea is known as *sasmita alam* (hints from nature) and such omens were generally thought to contain the most meaningful indications from which to deduce the lottery's outcome. When he was dressed in shorts, people would expect a low number; when he had gone to the movies, they wanted to know the number of the row and his seat, and so on. By interpreting his conduct, people were led to a number, while Pak Amat used the same technique to explain why he was always right. An exam-ple of his explanations runs as follows:

The outcome of the tail last week was 21. Why? Last Thursday, when I delivered my definitive speech about yesterday's outcome, my daughter was selling small tubes of sweets. I admonished you to buy them, because we should practise *gotong-royong* and help each other. It was on and in that tube of sweets that the outcome was revealed. On the tube you could read the words Fruit Drops and Fruit Norton. I told you not to use mystical parallel ciphers, but the straight numbers while adding and subtracting. You should have reasoned as follows: you noted 'Fruit Drops'; F means 7 if you read it in mirror-writing; then you have D, making 7D. D is the fourth letter of the alphabet. You add the numbers, which makes 11, which you add again, making 2. Fruit Norton is 76, because F is 7 and Norton is composed of 6 letters. You substract and find 1. The outcome must be 12 or 21, because there is left and right, hand and foot, male and female.

What's more, there were 12 sweets in the tube, again indicating 12 or 21. Besides this, the outcome of the week before was 87 for the 87th round of the national lottery. Last week was the 88th round, which was a clear indication, because 100 minus 88 makes 12. Of course, I do regret that I may not reveal the outcome itself. The army would come to arrest me if I did; I would bankrupt the bandar. Besides, it is not within the purposes of our government that I give straight numbers, because our government wants to stimulate its development efforts by way of the lottery. Yet, whoever has ears to hear, let him hear, and whoever has eyes to see, let him see.

The people who gathered around Pak Amat would acknowledge his unfathomable wisdom and hope that they would understand, too, 'when their time had come'.

Having learned the tricks of the trade, I decided that I would experiment with this thinking and act as a lottery predictor. Ever since I had interpreted the word 'Apollo', people would occasionally ask me for numbers, which I had, until then, refused. This experience was not unique: Catholic missionaries (foreign, white and celibate) also complained that they were asked for numbers, and that their behaviour was a source of inspiration for lottery prediction. Everything and everybody that is considered high, exalted, odd, peculiar, uncommon, may be regarded as an omen. In these latter senses, I certainly qualified. My credibility as a predictor was further enhanced by a reputation for mysticism and a strange way of life.

I acted on the following assumptions: I was peculiar and therefore revealing; things that were associated with me shared this quality, exposing cosmological coordination, or real co-incidence; such things might thus be interpreted as meaningful signs for the outcome of the lottery; because of this, people would be willing to sacrifice to obtain such meaningful signs from me. Subsequently, if asked for a number, I would offer such people a one-rupiah note (on which there is a number) for the sum of one hundred rupiahs. On a modest scale, this indeed appeared to work. After a few weeks, I stopped this practice, being satisfied at having tested a way of thinking.

These ideas of coordination, revealing form, and the absence of pure chance, reappear in all areas of Javanese life. The careful study of the structure of an event reveals its conditioning elements; these, in turn, are interpreted by way of classification, coordination, and intuitive reasoning. For instance, the sacrosanct date of independence, 17–8–1945, was no chance occurrence but a compelling co-incidence, a real *kebeneran*, because it was already written in the geographical coordinates of the country; in the way Sukarno spelled his name; in the structure of the Borobudur; in old prophecies. Similarly, there are the numbers 1 to 9 because there were nine Islamic apostles in Java; besides, the human body has nine openings. Being given the name Herman proved to be a preordained kebeneran, too, when he became, later in life, a favourite pupil of the deity-styled Manunggal sect leader, Romo Sumana. Their two names pair as hermana, *her* meaning *air* (water); *mana* meaning man, or Life. Hermono thus becomes the water of Life, or Life's essence. The meeting of guru Sumana and *dhalang* (puppeteer) Herman thus could not be a chance occurrence. It was a real co-incidence.

CHAPTER 3

The practice of mysticism

Contemporary mysticism is generically known as *kebatinan*. This word derives from the Arabic *batin* which means inner, in the heart, hidden and mysterious. Geertz interpreted batin to mean 'the inner realm of human experience'. Considering mysticism as an exponent of the priyayi style of life (the style of the refined man), he was struck by its empirical nature:

> The final appeal is always to (emotional) experience which carries its own meaning. God, forms of worship, and views of the nature of man, are always validated on these grounds — never on grounds of logic or essential rationality ... never on pure belief ... never in terms of social consequences ... but always on the quality of experience which is self-validating and empirical (1960:318).

While this may validly describe the experience of advanced mystics and masters, others are not so sure. Though kebatinan may be seen as development of the rasa, there appears to be an absence of agreement on the precise meaning, location, and potential of the batin, and many adepts even prefer to avoid the word kebatinan altogether. While this demonstrates the liveliness of the mystical scene, it also indicates a move away from the traditional quest for power, invulnerability and magical potency, to more psychological and spiritually oriented exercises. Whatever the case, kebatinan can safely be translated as 'science of the batin', mysticism, or Javanese science. Some people think it entails the essence of Javaneseness, even of being Indonesian.

> Kebatinan is the Indonesian way to happiness. In Indonesia, kebatinan, whatever it is called — *tasawuf* (Islamic mysticism), the science of perfection, theosophy, or mysticism — is a general phenomenon. Kebatinan develops the inner reality, the spiritual reality. Therefore, as long as the Indonesian people remain really Indonesian, possessed by their original identity, kebatinan will also certainly remain in Indonesia, whether within the official religions or outside of them (quoted in Subagyo 1973:133).

The practice of kebatinan is the quest for communication with ultimate reality; as a branch of knowledge, it studies man's place on earth and in the cosmos. It is based on the conviction of the essential oneness of all existence. The position of kebatinan is therefore more encompassing than the positions of Islam or Christianity that differentiate between the realms of God and man. Kebatinan mysticism views human existence in a cosmological context, making life itself a religious experience. In this view, it is not possible to separate the sacred from the profane; they all participate in the unity of existence.

The very notion of kebatinan implies that man has outward qualities and an inner potential, and that these two aspects are related. It is the moral task of all that exists to establish harmony between the outward lair and inner batin aspects of life, in the sense that the batin must master and guide the lair; then earthly life may harmonize and be in agreement with the principle of ultimate oneness. For this reason, social life has already been charted and laid down in the rules of etiquette and tradition, of formal religion and moral behaviour. All these regulate the known conditions and leave little room for adventure and further exploration. They are horizontal, known, clear, and fixed. The vertical relationships that are not of this world — that reveal 'the basic source and moral principle of Ketuhanan Yang Mahaesa',[4] or the Truth behind the obvious — are the really interesting field of activity and the essence of kebatinan.

The advanced mystics

Basically, the practice of mysticism is an individual endeavour. It is the lone search of man desiring reunification with his origin, aspiring to experience the revelation of the mystery of existence, or deliverance

---

4 In 1956, during the second BKKI congress, kebatinan was defined as 'the basic source and moral principle of Ke-Tuhanan Yang Maha Esa'. Although this definition is not very clear, it does contain some essential thinking about kejawèn mysticism: the human batin is the proof of the unity of existence, and the source of knowledge about it. Clearly, immanence goes all ways. This did not sit well with certain Muslim apologists, who concluded that the definition does not make sense, and that it should read the other way round: it is God that is the source of kebatinan.

from all earthly attachments. Many of the stories of shadow play mythology have this lonely quest as their subject. For instance, in the well-known story *Dewa Ruci*, the quest of Bima (one of the Pendawa brothers) to discover the essence of life, is vividly described. Similarly, the mystic is thought to tread a lone and dangerous path that may take him to the understanding and revelation of kasunyatan (Truth).

The mystical journey is most often thought to be performed in four stages, moving from the outside to the inside. Depending on whom one talks to, these stages may be described in various terms, Islamic or Javanese, but their meaning is the same. The lowest stage of the path (*saréngat*, or *shari'a*) is to respect and live according to religious rules and law. For the Muslim, this especially implies the faithful performance of the five daily prayers that serve to remind him of God, in the consciousness that all is in God's hands. The syncretist priyayi will refer to this stage as the faithful performance of duties, especially in the sense of respecting and honouring one's elders, one's guru, and one's king in the consciousness that to behave like that is to honour 'God'. Ordinary people will also stress respect for good order, but will not particularly emphasize the social hierarchy. Rather, they orient themselves to ancestors, spirits, the gods, and mythological heroes as the sources of power that need to be respected, again in the consciousness of respecting the great order.

Over the next three stages, the road narrows while moving away from the outward to the more inward and mystical. The adept gradually becomes aware that 'God is not to be met in Mecca but in the heart'. The second stage is known as *tarékat*, when the adept reflects upon the behaviour described in the first stage. By becoming conscious of its meaning, a person becomes aware, for instance, that ritual prayer is not just moving the body and reciting a formula, but a high and holy endeavour, and a basic preparation, to meet 'God' in one's innermost being.

The third stage, *hakékat*, is a confrontation with truth. It is the fully developed consciousness of the essence of prayer and service to 'God', the deep understanding that the only possible way of being is to be a servant of 'God', to be a dependent part in the great cosmic scheme. Regular prayer begins to lose its significance because life and behaviour become a permanent prayer to 'God'. Then personal life has become *laku* — attuned to and in step with Life. As a result, religious ritual as such has lost its meaning.

The last and highest stage is *makripat*, when the goal of concord between servant and Master *(jumbuhing kawula lan Gusti)* has been reached. At this stage, the individual soul has blended with the universal soul, and action has become pure laku, irrespective of what one does — work, meditate, defecate, sleep, or eat. At this point, the adept shines like the full moon over the earth, his very presence beautifying the world and inspiring others. He has become a representative of 'God' on earth.

To go this mystical way is strenuous, and requires a strong sense of purpose. One has to exercise in order to overcome one's lair aspects by means of *tapa* (asceticism), which may consist of fasting, praying, sexual abstinence, meditation, waking through the night, vigils at powerful grave sites, or retreating to mountains and into caves. The purpose of tapa is purification to reach *samadi*, which is a state of mind that can be described as a world-detached concentration, in which one is open to receive divine guidance and, ultimately, the revelation of the mystery of life, of origin and destination. Experienced mystics, however, will stress the discipline needed to reach samadi, and warn against the dangers of 'surfing' supernature when the results of ascetic practice are still insufficiently under control, or when the practice itself is aimed at magical purposes.

According to its objectives, Mangkunagara VII distinguished between four types of meditation, namely (1) to destroy by means of magic; (2) to attain a specific positive goal; (3) to experience revelation of the mystery of existence; (4) to be free from all earthly desires. These four types of concentration illustrate the wide range of mystical possibilities. The exercise of tapa and meditation are possible means to achieve purely worldly and magical purposes that may even be destructive to others, and that are clearly guided by egoistic motives, or *pamrih*. This type of mysticism is considered as sinful, as disturbing of cosmic order or divine will. It is 'black magic', and thus invites supernatural retaliation.

The second type of meditation, for the attainment of a positive goal, is also guided by the human will, and thus not free of pamrih. The opinions about its permissibility vary. Formerly, this type of 'white-magical' mysticism belonged to the tasks of the king, and when practised by or on behalf of the rulers, or in hands of concerned mystics, it is still thought to be a good thing.

The third and fourth types constitute the very purpose of mysticism, and correspond to the stages of hakékat and makripat respectively. These types of meditation are guided by the ideal 'to hear the divine voice', or 'the voice in the quiet'; they seek for the highest revelation, and thus require a constant purity of thought and deeds. Their accomplished practice is thought to be beneficial to society because it destroys evil and egoism, and thus spreads justice and well-being.

Because of these various potentials, it is hard to draw the line between magical mysticism and the practice of pure kebatinan. By way of tapa and samadi man can penetrate the cosmos and acquire power and inspiration from higher forces. He may also consciously relate to any of the lower supernatural beings, such as the souls of ancestors, the various heroes of the shadow play, devils and angels, gods, ghosts and spirits. Even while striving for a pure mystical experience, he may be led astray on his journey because he may be guided by unconscious impure motives, or because his laku is still wanting, or his tapa for self-purification insufficient.

In order to advance on the path to mystical union, the mystic should live up to two basic injunctions. The first is the caution against egoistic motives, which means not claiming for oneself what has been obtained or revealed. After all, man is nothing; he is powerless; he is a mere exponent of Life that encompasses all. Because he will, nevertheless, find that his mystical advance increases his powers and understanding, the second prohibition is against pride in achievement, and proclaiming that one knows. The results of the practice of mysticism should remain a secret between mystical servant and Master.

Socially, the adepts should faithfully fulfil their *darma* (duty), and *nrima*, that is accept their station in life and their fate with an attitude of grateful acceptance. By fulfilling their task in this world, people honour 'God'. It is a first step towards the mystical goal. To live according to duty and the rules of social order is to fulfil the will of 'God' and to shape one's destiny; it is a form of elementary laku, in this case, to enact the nothingness of man, and to be an instrument of 'God'.

The mystical master

Often kejawèn people think kebatinan involves far more than mysticism. They see it as a style of life that is not necessarily religious or mystical, but which entails the development of the inner being for the sake of the mastery of self and social life. In this understanding, the cultivation of equanimity and a strong batin may have little to do with the practice of mysticism. For most, though, the idea of kebatinan is associated with its mystical and magical potential.

Treading the mystical path is a dangerous and difficult endeavour. One may become possessed by evil forces, go mad, or be led astray. People should certainly not engage in it at too young an age, when one is thought to be unable to muster the necessary discipline over body and spirit. People are, therefore, well advised to associate themselves with a guru, a master who is thought to have advanced along the path, and who is willing to initiate other people in his *ngèlmu* (esoteric knowledge).

Most accomplished individual mystics do not aspire to become gurus, and the second mystical injunction, against pride in achievement, strongly counteracts aspirations to that role. At best, they will initiate their sons, to whom they may pass on their ngèlmu, but they will avoid the limelight. Research among the individual mystics was therefore fairly difficult. They tended to avoid publicity, to view their practice as a purely individual affair, and they considered their knowledge as a secret science.

Naturally, established *guru kebatinan*, or mystical masters, were easier to get at, although it generally took some time and a good introduction before they were convinced of the sincerity of the noninitiated researcher. If the latter was taken seriously, having demonstrated his willingness to learn and to participate in mystical exercises, the doors swung open to the observation of kebatinan mysticism.

The practice of kebatinan can best be observed through participation in the *aliran kebatinan* (mystical groups or sects), with which many Javanese have some experience or other. Invariably, these groups grow around the person of a guru. His science, or ngèlmu, may have been taught to him by his father or another guru, or may derive from the study of Javanese ethical and mystical literature. But the real source of his knowledge is his *wahyu*, the revelation he received as a result of his successful and conscientious practice of the mystical discipline.

Because of this latter characteristic, Javanese mysticism lacks a systematic theology, and the theories, practices, and methods of advancing along the mystical path vary considerably among the sects. Most guru stress the originality of their revelations or intuitive insights while denying knowledge from books or the influence of tradition. They feel that they start anew, and most aliran kebatinan do not survive the death of their originators for long. It follows that present kebatinan mysticism is characterized by an absence of uniform rules, a paucity of systematic conceptualization, and a proliferation of terms and concepts.

Be that as it may, there is a marked tendency towards institutionalization, because some mystical masters have recorded their revelations and secretive knowledge in writing, enabling their followers to organize themselves, and to perpetuate their teachings after their death. Mystical movements of a national scope, such as Pangestu, Subud, Sapta Darma, and Sumarah, exemplify this; all of them are in their third or fourth generation now. Some mystical movements even survive in spite of their oral tradition. Cases in point are the Islamic *tarékat* (mystical brotherhoods), in which the holy formulae and methods are transmitted from master to a favourite pupil. A notable peasant group to survive since the end of the nineteenth century consists of followers of the teachings of Surontiko Samin.

Whatever the case may be, a master should possess certain qualities if he wants to attract followers. He should be recognized to have achieved an advanced stage of mysticism, and thus possess a wahyu. He should have an aura of mystery and knowledge, yet also lead a responsible life, be able to stand worldly suffering, possess equanimity of spirit, and be a real father-figure for his followers. As long as a guru possesses all these qualities, he will be believed, honoured, and obeyed; his advice will be taken as inspired words. On the other hand, the master who does not live up to his teachings, or who abuses his position of trust, may easily lose his followers.

Apart from explaining and guiding mystical exercises, masters tend to be more than teachers only. They should be patrons, fathers, that is real *bapak*, in relation to their clients. They should advise them, cure their illnesses, make calculations, give predictions and, above all, they should function as intermediaries between their followers and the realm of spirits, ancestors, and 'God'. In spite of all these services, they should not expect material rewards: they should be without self-interest, and care for their own livelihood. Followers may bring food, cigarettes, some money, sacred objects, and other useful things to show their respect and honour their guru, but gurus themselves may never ask, and are expected to be available to tend to the needs and sufferings of their followers.

At this point it is politic to distinguish the guru kebatinan from other practitioners of Javanese esoterism, such as *dhukun*. Mystical masters see themselves as *sepuh*, or *wong tuwa* — respected and respectable elders whose wisdom, revealed wahyu, and benevolent inclinations make them father-figures in relation to those who depend on their insights and advice. The source of their wisdom is with and within themselves. In this sense, they are very different from dhukun who are basically shamans, people who go into trance, who are possessed by spirits, and who cultivate contacts with an underworld of black-magical forces. Their power comes from without; they do not harbour power within the own person. Besides, they exercise their craft for a fee; they are not free of pamrih such as the mystical teacher should be.

Whatever the case, in ordinary life mystical masters may be found among all professions. They may be automobile mechanics, farmers, university professors, members of the armed forces, physicians, judges, politicians, engineers, or teachers. Often they are markedly extrovert, and virtually all of them show the self-confidence of persons who are in close contact with higher reality. Most are convinced of their mission and the uniqueness of their teachings; in spite of their secular activities, they tend to explain worldly events, especially politics and personal experiences, from a cosmological and symbolic perspective.

The practice in the aliran kebatinan

During the period of post-war florescence, several of the aliran kebatinan have expanded to become national associations that claim up to hundred thousand members. Others are of strictly local significance, and may be as small as several tens of members. Local kebatinan meetings tend to be held in small groups (five to fifty participants) around the person of a master or his deputy. These groups tend to be rather homogeneous in status, although some aliran draw their members from all strata of society.

Basically, aliran kebatinan serve as schools for the individual to learn to tread the path of mysticism; this individual goal is clearly recognized. Kebatinan, in all its variations, is a culture of the inner man, developing the intuitive inner feeling, or rasa, and inner tranquility. The common method of reaching this is known as *sujud*, literally, 'to prostrate oneself before God', but here meaning, 'to surrender oneself to God's will'. It is during this self-surrender that a person may intuitively experience the presence of 'God' in the inner being. This mystical communion is essentially a free-floating and undirected process, in which the initiative to make itself felt lies with the other side. The quality of this contact depends on the state of preparation and purification of the individuals concerned.

It is recognized that it is difficult to establish communion with the sphere of 'God'. The kebatinan adepts have to bring their self-surrender to perfection by training and exercising their rasa. This explains why the sessions are often referred to as *latihan* (exercise) or *olah rasa* (training of the rasa). Their content and form vary widely among the different aliran and gurus. They may be patterned upon the Islamic prayer ritual, such as prostrating oneself before God — while concentrating on the rasa — or after the Muslim mystical exercise of repeated recitation of God's name, known as *dikir*. Other aliran may practise silent prayer, or short concentration exercises, while others still engage in ecstatic shaking sessions that may last for almost half an hour. Generally, the exercise to establish contact with the sphere of 'God' — generically referred to as sujud — will last from five to ten minutes. Whatever form it takes, it is the enactment of surrendering oneself to 'God', often accompanied by the formula, 'I am not capable of anything; I do not pretend to be anything'.

The mysticism that is practised in the groups does not foster the strong mental discipline that is required of the individual mystic who pursues tapa and lonely meditation throughout the night. Normally, the guru will acknowledge the value of minor forms of tapa as a good preparation for sujud, but he will caution his pupils against samadi proper, because it is intrinsically dangerous, and requires lengthy preparation and experience. Besides, the ordinary aliran members do not aspire to reach high levels of mysticism. To them, it is highly satisfying to sit at the feet of their guru and to 'bathe', as it were, in his charisma; to listen to his inspired words; and to communally associate with the fascinating realm of supernature in an esoteric milieu of initiated friends.

Generally, kebatinan meetings take place in the home of the guru. Both men and women come together, and people of all ages may participate. Typically, adherents of various denominations, such as Islam, Christianity, Buddhism, combine. When everybody is present, the meeting opens with a *sujud pengheningan*, that is, a sujud exercise to establish clarity of mind and concentration. After this preparation, the guru speaks about the meaning of life according to his insights. Then those present may be invited to question the guru.

The formal part of the meeting is the latihan, or olah rasa. Led by their master, those present will sujud and surrender themselves in order to open up to higher reality. Thereafter, those present are invited to talk about their inner experiences during this sujud, to ask questions about it, and tell what they have heard, felt, seen, and experienced. One by one, the guru will answer the questions and explain the experiences. Upon this, the master may relate his personal practice, explain kebatinan and sujud, and give advice on questions of everyday life. After all this, the formal meeting is closed with a short sujud, in order to reassert the consciousness that man is nothing in the eyes of God, and that people should be well aware of themselves and their actions. Subsequently, the gathering may remain together and chat about mystical experiences, mysterious happenings, the national lottery, and other things that are beyond common sense.

The atmosphere of kebatinan gatherings tends to be cosy, intimate, and spontaneous. The mood is one of fellowship and brotherhood, easing over status differences and fostering oneness of feeling. The guru often forms the marked exception and holds a position of reverence. During the formal latihan, the emphasis is on intuition and feeling. This means, among others, that people should free themselves from their common sense and rationality. The latter belong to the body, and thus tie the person to the physical world. It is through the rasa that man can bridge the distance to 'God', and acknowledge the divine presence in his batin.

Whatever the guru says during the latihan is considered to be inspired word. The mood is essentially one of nonrationality and fantasy, and that mood is refreshing. It is living in the all-possible, where one has been freed from the ordinary laws of gravity and an often weary existence. And while the world of everyday life becomes inconsequential, symbols become real; where words create a new reality, the objective world of sense perception becomes illusory. Kebatinan mysticism is a surrender to nonobjective reality and intuition.

Besides the intimacy and the nonrationality of kebatinan meetings, the high emotional tension of the participants is noteworthy. This is, for instance, apparent from the uncontrolled volume of voice during dikir exercises; from the loud and spontaneous laughter as a reaction to absurdities; from uncontrolled movements of the body, crying, and the intense relaxation after the latihan. Entering a new reality by way of kebatinan may transform the entire personality. Another striking characteristic is the commitment to the charismatic master, and the emotional ties among members. Often, attachment to the guru becomes more important than loyalty to parents or family. As a result, some gurus may wield much influence over their followers.

Because of these various characteristics, such as release of tension; temporary escape from oppressive social ties; esoteric community; experience of inner tranquillity, and trust in the father-figure of the guru, certain psychiatrists believe the practice of kebatinan to be beneficial to mental health. Yet, because mysticism may entail far more than the release experience during kebatinan meetings, others are not so sure. Practising physicians seem to agree, though, that living according to the Javanese wisdom of acceptance of life as it comes; of cultivating equanimity; of avoiding upset, are conducive to psychological well-being.

Mystical reasoning

Javanese mystical reasoning often draws parallels with the shadow play mythology to explain events and conditions in the here-and-now. When the representatives of anarchy are in ascendency, life on earth is in disorder; contrarily, peace and happiness will prevail when the forces of order reign. Life on earth is coordinated with cosmic happenings —

much in the sense of horoscopy — and man can only accept life as pre-ordained by fate. After all, life on earth is but a mirror image of prevailing cosmic conditions.

Upon deeper reflection, however, this relationship reveals itself as two-sided. When the spiritual condition of man is orderly and quiet, when he is not guided by his passions and personal desires, life on earth will be just and prosperous, which in its turn reflects an orderly cosmos and harmony between 'God' and men.

Upon deeper reflection still, it is man himself who holds the key to his condition. In mysticism and magic, he may relate to the representatives of order or of anarchy. Basically, the cosmos is morally neutral and man is the cause of his own condition. Although most kejawèn people vaguely believe in the law of karma and the possibility of reincarnation, these beliefs do not strongly influence their temporary aspirations. Life is in the here-and-now. The important things are, therefore, the moral and spiritual conditions of persons and society, which in their turn cause the state of affairs, in the world as well as at a cosmological level, to assume the form they have.

These three levels of rationalization are variously used to explain whatever happens. Yet, in all the three types of explanation, it is clear that the cause of events lies in their structure. The simplest examples of the first line of reasoning, namely, that the supernatural situation conditions events on earth, lie in the use of *primbon* (magical almanacs) and *pétungan* (calculations). For instance, if a man wants to steal a cow, he consults the primbon. To be successful, he may read that on *Selasa-Kliwon* (a combination of the seven and five day weeks — such days occur once every thirty-five days), it is right to move in north-easterly direction, for a distance of five miles or two villages, where he should take a black cow (perhaps he needs a new moon in addition, the company of a friend, and suchlike). If he acts accordingly, his self-confidence may be boosted and contribute to the success of the mission. If the police know the primbon too, they may trace the thief by interpreting it in reverse.

The pétungan are used like the primbon, but may consist of fresh calculations in order to find the right marriage partner, the date, and the hour of a ceremony, or when to start building a town hall. They are, like the primbon, a means of coordinating earthly events with cosmic conditions. A fine example is the lay-out of the first eight-year development plan of 1960, which was construed after the auspicious formula 17–8–1945 (the date of the declaration of independence) in 17 chapters, 8 volumes, and 1945 clauses. Such coordination evokes the right conditions; the plan becomes a mantra, 'self-implementing' so to speak. This example also partly illustrates the second way of reasoning, namely that the conditions of man and supernature are interdependent, without any possibility of establishing the primacy of causes. This type of reasoning comes to the fore most clearly in shadow play performances. *Wayang* shadow theatre is seen as the projection of cosmic conditions on earth, yet the choice of a certain episode is in the hands of man. For instance, a committee of Yogyanese notables had decided that they would, for once, stage the various episodes of the great war as recorded in the *Mahabharata*. The plays were performed in succession once every three weeks. On the evening of Saturday, 30 November 1957, the story was staged in which the hero Karno perishes. That same evening, disgruntled students from Bima, Sumbawa, threw five grenades at President Sukarno, who was popularly known as *Bung* (Brother) Karno. To these Yogyanese gentlemen, this event demonstrated the danger of projecting this violent mythology into the world; doing so may release untamed cosmic forces with unknown but perilous consequences.

The story of the conjuring of a plague of mice bears comparison. In those days, President Sukarno had launched, in Yogyakarta, his campaign for the recovery of then Dutch New Guinea. He decided on that city, because he needed the help of the spirit army of *Nyai* Loro Kidul, the powerful Queen of the Southern Ocean. Through her help, he was successful. However, when Western New Guinea became part of the Indonesian territory, Sukarno failed to pay tribute to the Nyai and, therefore, the spirits that had been recruited to recover the new province could not find their way back to their aquatic origin. Roaming around in the Yogyakarta area, they caused havoc to the rice harvest. Because of this, the mayor of Yogyakarta ordered the performance of the powerful shadow play *Semar Boyong* on the mystically potent beach of Parangtritis. In this way, the Queen was acknowledged, and her army could retire to its realm. The plague abated. Similarly, the politically powerful may still order certain energy-laden shadow performances to achieve their political designs.

The practice of mysticism itself provides the best illustration of the third form of reasoning, namely, that man himself causes conditions on earth by his moral and spiritual behaviour. Through ascetic exercises, a person prepares him or herself to make contact with supernatural agents. These are liable both to the conscious will and subconscious intentions of the adept, at the same time that the penetration of super-nature results in enhancing his power. Because of this, a mystic or magician can influence events in the here-and-now by the imposition of his will and manipulation of supernatural forces. In this way, a person can even temporarily suspend his *karma* (cosmologically conditioned fate) and influence *kodrat* ('the will of God'). Such practices are thought to be a grave sin, but are, nevertheless, well within human possibility.

The kebatinan-klenik controversy

If man is the ultimate cause of his condition, his moral and spiritual behaviour should be watched. The control of spiritual behaviour belongs to the tasks of Pakem and the Ministry of Religion. The Ministry should also foster the conscientious practice of the recognized religions, because when all men faithfully follow their religious injunctions, life in society will be harmonious. It is this very thinking about the importance of moral and spiritual behaviour that causes most of the controversy between religion and mysticism, and also between kebatinan and its klenik expressions.

The theory of mysticism is a theory of magic, and it is difficult to draw a clear line between what is mystically permissible and what is sinful. We have seen that asceticism and samadi meditation, with the purpose of effecting a good result in society, are generally thought to be permissible, even if such practices are not free from self-interest. In the old days, they belonged to the tasks of the king, as a matter of course. Yet, are such practices permissible among ordinary people? May one, for instance, use the power one derives from mysticism to cure people? Among the bigger national aliran, Sapta Darma and Susila Budi Dharma (Subud) hold it to be an obligation for their advanced members to heal people through the practice of mystical surrender and prayer. To others, curing practices are totally taboo, not because they are impossible, but because they will cause feelings of pride. The purist and intellectual Paguyuban Ngèsti Tunggal (Pangestu) strongly warns against the dangers of interfering in the 'Godly' ordained order of events, and has even outlawed trust in the power of heirlooms and graves.

Another controversial issue concerns the permissibility of giving predictions, especially of lottery numbers. The general opinion is that lottery prediction constitutes an abuse of mystical power, because the lottery very clearly relates to greed and money. This connection with the lowly passions and the material world makes lottery prediction a klenik, a black-magical practice. Still, some guru reason that the exploitation of their mystical powers helps their followers to survive, while they themselves are without self-interest in the outcome of the lottery. Whether defending prediction or objecting to the practice, nobody denies the possibility of prediction. By practising tapa and samadi, a person may acquire insight into future events, but the mystical admonishment against pride and self-satisfaction warns against the dissemination of these insights. A person still proclaiming such knowledge is mystically sinful.

Klenik practices demonstrate that one has been led astray, that one is inspired by lowly passions and materialism, and guided by the spiritual underworld. Such practices are thought to be harmful to the nation and to cause social instability; they are, therefore, illegal. It is the task of Pakem to see to it that aliran or persons who engage in klenik manipulations are prosecuted, and cease their harmful activities. Yet it is difficult to separate the pure kebatinan from the klenik. Orthodox Islam may see all mysticism as heresy, and condemn it as klenik. Some purist kebatinan groups are quick to denounce others as deviants. The decision to disband aliran kebatinan, and to prosecute its members, lies with Pakem. Generally Pakem takes action only when certain groups are suspected of being infiltrated by communists; when their practices result in bodily harm or death; or when they engage in anti-Islamic activities. In Pakem's view, practices are klenik when they threaten to upset social order.

CHAPTER 4

Ethics and social philosophy

Ethics

In 1955, at the first Congress of Indonesian Mystics, the BKKI, the ethics of kebatinan were formulated as, *Sepi ing pamrih, ramé ing gawé. Mamayu hayuning Buwono.* The first two elements of this formula combine as an often-heard kejawèn maxim, that probably enjoys a Java-wide popularity. Their approximate translation is: 'Unselfish, diligent'. The third element roughly reads as, 'To beautify the World'. It is of interest to note that the formula was rendered in Javanese, whereas the language of the minutes of the congress was Indonesian. This was not because the formula cannot be 'translated', but because virtually all literal translations have to fail since they will miss the proverbial, the cultural point.

The first element, sepi ing pamrih — to be unselfish, not to be driven by the desire for personal gain — contains a key to kejawèn wisdom. It stands for the conscious control of one's passions, because these stand in the way of achieving a quiet heart. In Indonesian translation, pamrih is often rendered as *kepentingan diri*, or self-interest and self-importance. From the Javanese viewpoint, the self, the body and personal ambitions, should be overcome; they are hindrances on the way to fulfilment. If these barriers are succesfully surmounted, it will result in a benevolent attitude toward others, and to mankind in general.

This latter attitude is a consequence of being sepi ing pamrih, and not a purpose in itself. When self-interest has been overcome and a pure mind established, when people have the correct attitudes, conditions in this world will follow. It is self-interest that stands in the way of a good world and a pure life. When people strive to better themselves, they improve worldly conditions as a result. Yet, the purpose of kebatinan is to build a harmonious relationship with 'God', irrespective of mundane consequences.

For this reason, it is questionable when the second clause, ramé ing gawé, is interpreted to mean 'to actively perform good deeds for the benefit of all'. Ramé may doubtlessly be translated as 'active', or even 'with gusto', but the word gawé refers to 'work' which, in the kejawèn context means station in life. It therefore means 'to be a good servant', to faithfully and actively perform one's task in the social hierarchy. It is a fulfilling of one's task, of the obligations of one's destined place. Therefore, I prefer to interpret ramé ing gawé as 'the faithful practice of one's duty in the place where one has to perform — be it as a peasant or a servant, a functionary or a king — not emphasizing personal initiative or responsibility but the sincere acceptance of one's place in life'.

The third element of the formula, mamayu hayuning Buwono, has been elegantly translated as 'to adorn the world'. This renders its meaning much more precisely than the proposal to Indonesianize it as 'to actively strive after the well-being of the world in general'. There is no activity implied in the idea mamayu hayuning Buwono. To do this means a bow to modern thinking about progress and development that misses the kebatinan point. Fighting pamrih is beneficial, but the idea that one should be a mystic to better the world is entirely fallacious. Cause and effect follow each other, but are not equivalent to purpose, and beneficial worldly consequences are entirely secondary, mere consequences, that are irrelevant to the mystical quest per se.

The noble aim of kebatinan is to achieve unity with higher reality through overcoming the self. This very act denies worldly purpose. It is personal fulfilment through becoming fully attuned to 'God', to Life. Whereas the way to such fulfilment may begin with elementary worldly steps, such as respect for the social order, the very practice of mysticism aims at giving up worldly attachments. The first steps had, therefore, better be seen as the training of selflessness. Thus, even if the worldly consequences were not beneficial, the mystical ethic would not be different.

The dominant idea in mysticism as practised in Yogyakarta is to be sepi ing pamrih. This 'selflessness' is implemented through the advice to practise values such as *rila* (nonattachment), nrima (gratefully accepting life as it comes), *waspada-éling* (mindfulness), *andap-asor* (humility), *prasaja* (modesty), and *sabar* (patience). Another way is 'to be concerned', to exercise solicitude, known as *pribatin*, which many people give shape to through minor ascetic observances. Altogether, these express a personal reaction to the insecurities and precariousness of existence, but they do not constitute a conscious endeavour to better it. The teachings of the lowbrow mystical groups express this thinking best. In the spirit of surrendering everything to 'God', they pronounce dictums such as, 'I am not capable of anything; I do not possess anything'. Their worldly ethic is simply formulated as, 'not to harm one's fellows'. People should have a good attitude toward one another, make each other happy, and refrain from disturbing each other's peace of mind.

There is nothing particularly mystical about this. People in general appreciate feeling at peace, not being bothered, and often evaluate personal life, and that in the neighbourhood, in terms of its *tata-tentrem* (quiet orderliness). For this purpose — for the sake of inner harmony — social life appears to be somewhat overregulated. The rules of etiquette, that is, *tatakrama* ('the order of good manners'), shape interpersonal behaviour. *Tatacara* ('the order of custom') moulds communal behaviour. Religious ritual fashions the formal relationship between God and man. Self-control masters human drives and emotions. All this regulation is thought to be fundamentally important for maintaining and enjoying an harmonious existence. The breach of such harmony, the disturbance of that quiet order, is humanly wrong, because it is socially dangerous, and ultimately sinful. In terms of worldly action, kebatinan, therefore, emphasizes the exercise of right behaviour as a conscious endeavour. This ethic is neither this-worldly nor other-worldly, but directed to the harmony of the totality of existence, of life within Life.

Social philosophy

Unity and harmony

The mystical ideal of unity and harmony between man and 'God' stands as the model for the relationship between man and society. The quest for unity-harmony, and the maintenance of order, are the predominant elements. The idea of unity implies orderliness. Personal desires, ambitions, and passions are thought to endanger harmony, and thus it is thought that 'to sacrifice for the sake of social harmony will lead to the highest rewards': a person should give himself up to the community rather than try to impose his will.

Javanese education tries to instil these ideas. To be Javanese is to be cultured. It means to know civilized manners and to be conscious of social position. A 'recognized' Javanese is a person who knows order. As a result, the child is considered to be *durung jawa*, not yet Javanese, not yet cultured. The child is a person who does not yet know its manners and place in the order. To the Javanese *budaya* ('culture') is not a vague anthropological notion. Budaya implies being civilized, in other words, wise: conscious of self, place, and manners; conscious of self and others. To have budaya is to have 'graduated' from durung jawa to *wis jawa* (to have become Javanese). It is to know and show appropriate manners, to speak the right words, to maintain an orderly existence, and to respect the social hierarchy.

Conversely, disorder, discord and unruliness are distasteful. According to the notions of kebatinan, order and equilibrium are upset by selfishness and passions; according to the notions of society, the upset is caused by the pursuit of personal interests and ambitions. Society should be shielded from the drives and emotions of unruly individuals.

As long as children are considered to be durung jawa, they get their way. They are nursed and nurtured with indulgence, and shielded from startling experiences. Tolerance and indulgence, in their turn, safeguard their surroundings from being upset by children's yet uncivilized tempers and behaviour. Gradually, children become 'human', become Javanese. In the process, they have to learn to distinguish between themselves and the interests of family and wider community. Individual and society are subsequently shielded from each other by the internalization of all those rules and regulations that are thought to guarantee correct social form, irrespective of personal wishes.

Relationships should be agreeable, peaceful and friendly, demonstrating unity of purpose. In brief, they should be characterized by the spirit of *rukun*. This rich Malay and Javanese concept has been glossed as 'to be in harmony', 'quiet and peaceful', 'like the ideal relationship of friendship', 'without quarrel and strife', 'friendly', and 'united in purpose while mutually helping each other'. Ideally, communal life should be informed by the spirit of rukun, implying the smoothing over of differences, cooperation, mutual acceptance, and willingness to compromise. And, hopefully, life in society will be as life in the ideal community.

Ideologically, the value of rukun is saliently expressed in the ideals of mutual assistance and the sharing of burdens, known as *gotong-royong*, and the process of decision-making by mutual consultation, known as *musyawarah*. Ideally, musyawarah is a procedure in which all voices and opinions are heard. All these are considered to be equally respectable, and to contribute to the solution sought. Musyawarah seeks to establish 'the totality of the will' of the deliberating group, then to formulate a unanimous decision, called *mufakat*. This completeness and unanimity is a guarantee for truth and right decision making; truth is contained in the unity of the group.

Hierarchy

With its origin in Muslim-style deliberations, musyawarah easily evokes an image of equality, of the equal worth of opinions and of participants. In the Javanese case, this idea of the equality of people 'in the eyes of God' — thus moral equality — is strange at the very least. More than strange, it is disturbing. To the extent that people are morally unequal, to the same extent is hierarchy the backbone of social organization. Similar to the ideas underlying the working of an army, clear hierarchical organization guarantees order, is conducive to avoiding open conflict, and serves predictability.

Moral inequality comes naturally. People are born unequal. This is immediately clear when we reflect on the positions of dependent children and providing parents. Nor is this in dispute with the kebatinan point of view. While all people comprise an outward and an inner aspect, and all have a sixth sense, namely, the intuitive rasa, this does not mean that all develop in the same way. Some people are entirely worldly, their lair aspect apparently dominating their lives. Others, such as kebatinan adepts, may prioritize the growth of their batin, and train their inner feeling in order to be sensitive to the presence of 'God'. Some people merely pursue their self-interest, while others seek to accomplish themselves through sacrificing for the welfare of society. In view of all this, who is to argue for people's basic moral equality?

Javanese life seems to move between the poles of grossness and refinement, with the latter seen as more desirable, more civilized. If this refinement concerns more than outward form alone — if it is really part of personality — people will clearly be recognized as morally superior. This notwithstanding, in practical life, all social relationships are hierarchically ordered in fine nuances of relative status. The very use of the Javanese language, and its concomitant manners, clearly expresses this. It is impossible to speak Javanese without reference to the position of the person spoken to in relation to the position of the speaker. In its many complicated and formal gradations, the choice of words reflects position, intimacy or formality, age, social distance and rank, together with all the nuances of relative expectations, obligations, and rights. The choice of words and language are expressive of the prevailing order.

Language and manners serve to express *hormat*, the respect and honour to which the other person is entitled. They express the ideal of maintaining the correct social form and ordered relationships. This idealization of order is best served if people adapt themselves to the prevailing circumstances. People should know their place and task, should honour and respect those who are in higher positions, while being benevolent towards, and responsible for, those who are in lower positions. If all people lived according to their station and task in life, a harmonious hierarchical society, complete in itself, would follow; its very harmony demonstrating the favour of the gods.

This in itself shows that respect for hierarchy is moral behaviour per se, and that hierarchical order is moral, too. If kings, or leaders, fathers and superiors — those who are entitled to exercise power — maintain order, they do the right thing, even if the measures they take can be rated as gross. It is their task to restore order, to restore the semblance of harmony.

Individual and society

Life in Javanese society does not seem to leave much room for individual expression. It somehow isolates people from each other. Personal expression — especially the show of emotions — is impolite, embarrassing, and a violation of the privacy of others. Social life should be shielded from individual intrusions by safeguarding polite form, hierarchy, and harmony. These keep the individual and society at a distance from each other. People may, and should, hide behind formality and politeness. Good manners are evasive manners; one should say 'yes' because agreement is polite. One should not involve the self, but maintain form, and suppress personal needs.

To the people of South-Central Java, refined manners and indirectness are important. They are signs of self-mastery and patience, protective of one's self, while slowly moving to one's goal. Often they jokingly observe: 'Suppose that you want to go to Yogya, that's your purpose. In that case, you should go to Surabaya first, then to Jakarta, back to Semarang, and by way of Banyumas you will surely get to Yogya'. It is not important to arrive there as soon as possible; the important thing is that you get there, precisely and on target. Look which way the cat will jump before you make your move, take your time, and be alert to the intentions of others while remaining discreet about your own.

With all this in mind, it is small wonder that ethics are largely formulated in terms of don'ts rather than of do's. The cardinal command is *tepa slira* ('to measure by oneself') what result one's words and actions will have on the feelings of others. In other words, do as you would be done by. In practice, this usually comes out in terms of, 'Do not irritate the other'; 'Be careful not to hurt the other's feeling'; 'Do not insult the other but show respect for his position'; 'Do not cause trouble to others'; 'Stay away where you have no business'; 'Be careful not to cause the other loss of face', and suchlike, which all boil down to a self-protective strategy of restraint. Not to involve oneself is wise and good.

This rather self-centred ethic combines with a sensitivity to personal honour. For that, one is of course dependent on the perceptions of others. Besides, being well-regarded and receiving honour also results in obligations, since status depends on the personal effort to live up to expectations. Especially if sufficiently high up, 'One has no place to hide one's face', and irrespective of — possibly disastrous — financial consequences, the need is felt to demonstrate status by throwing a big, lavish party on the occasion of major life-cycle rituals, especially circumcisions and nuptials. When I remarked to my landlady that a wedding at one of her neighbours had been quite impressive, with around two-hundred guests, her spontaneous reaction was that she had entertained at least five hundred people when her daughter married, thus belittling the status of the next-door family.

With status considerations apparently so central to life in Yogya, the question of self-respect naturally presented itself. It became especially intriguing when I checked on the translations of self-esteem *(eigenwaarde)* and self-respect *(zelfrespect)* in a recent Dutch-Indonesian dictionary. In Indonesian, the word self-esteem was glossed as *harga diri*, while self-respect was rendered as *harga diri yang wajar*, 'genuine value of the self', which is a description rather than a translation. Subsequently, I went in search of Javanese interpretations.

The vast majority of my kejawèn respondents thought the Indonesian notion of harga diri to correspond with *praja*, the prestige that results from one's *pangkat* (status position). In trying to differentiate this from the Dutch notion of self-respect, almost all of them stuck to the Javanese idea of praja, some of them explaining that the idea of harga diri was typical of Sumatrans, who could not appreciate the important value of humility. In their view, self-esteem and self-respect meant the same thing, namely, to be well-regarded, and to receive the honour due to one's status. In other words, self-respect appeared to stand for what other people consider a person to be; in social life, that becomes one's identity. Outwardly, therefore, the individual equates with his position and identifies with the prestige that others attribute to it.

Of the twenty informants questioned about self-respect, three gave kebatinan-related answers, differentiating the notion of the 'true I' from the visible person, while only three others differentiated it in a clear social perspective. Two of them were members of the modern Muslim association Muhammadiyah, the other being well-known as a flagrantly independent-minded artist. Although these three agreed that to most the idea of harga diri was dependent on status recognition and attributed honour, they also recognized a more personal variant of self-respect. They expressed the individual-centred notion as *kaprawiran* or *kasatriyan*, meaning to have the courage to go one's own way, irrespective of the opinion of others, to live according to the own convictions and mission in life. They referred to the Prophet and the Muslim saints, or to the mythological heroes Bima and Karno, as the examples to follow.

In a further attempt to clarify the issue, I tried to find an equivalent for the western notion of conscience. The idea is often translated as *suara batin* (inner voice) which relates fundamentally to mysticism and intuition. It certainly does not convey the idea of a personal superego. Although the Javanese notion of *rumangsaning ati* seems to come somewhat closer, it clearly remains a form of sensitivity regarding others or, as one informant explained: 'It is a feeling deeper than shame that has to be trained in order to develop into a fine sense as to what might hurt others'. Along with several people later interviewed, he disagreed that it would be reluctance to do wrong per se, or in the eyes of 'God'; he also rejected the idea that actions are good or bad in themselves. According to him, and all other kejawèn informants, a good or bad action always relates to deeds done unto others.

Infraction of the social rules is not intrinsically bad, and one may think whatever one likes, as long as one visibly conforms to the demands of social life. It is bad when infractions are noted, and one should abstain from such actions because people may see them. Conscience is consciousness of others, of the eyes, comments, and criticism that affect one's position and respect for one's status. A good person is generally described as a person who knows the feeling of shame and who fears the opinion of others. Apparent conformity with the demands of one's group is the basis of good conscience. In effect, this means refraining from actions that would not be tolerated by one's fellows, and that would thus threaten personal quiet; even then, such actions are seen as not so much bad as plainly stupid.

To hold a different opinion or to act in a different manner when out of eyesight or earshot, are accepted, and often even expected. To cheat, be corrupt, frequent prostitutes, and the like, when far away, are personal matters that do not concern one's fellows as long as it is done discreetly. Such actions merely concern relationships with irrelevant outsiders. Life in the outside world has no connexion with private existence, and I have often been amazed by the licentiousness of people freed from the pressure to conform, such as is imposed in ordinary life.

Persons out beyond the bounds set by relevant others are considered to be bags full of emotions and passions that will run wild once given the opportunity. It is, therefore, good to be, and feel, controlled by those others. Conscious of the formal rules of social life, they have the compass bearings to sail on; should these rules break down, people may lose both orientation and sense of proportion. It is therefore wise to guard honour and prestige, and to avoid scandal under all circumstances. If persons feel immune to this because of their position of power, they may become very unscrupulous and threatening characters indeed.

Apparently, the claims of society concern the lair, that is visible behaviour and outward appearance. These social claims pervade social life, and most people appear to feel secure through living up to these demands. People are entitled to entertain whatever personal opinions, thoughts and emotions they like, as long as they accept and conform to public demands. They are expected to shape social life through mastering impulses and by presenting themselves in an elegant, subdued and accomplished manner. To many or most, such successful role-playing is a great source of satisfaction in itself.

This gratification does not come for free, however, but is the outcome of constant efforts to take the desires of others into account. In social life, one can never really take it easy, always having to stand on tiptoe, as it were, to be cautious and conscious of the impression made on others. As a result, life is never really relaxing. It is precisely this that constitutes one of the attractions of kebatinan, in which people can freely create a world where they have been freed from social demands. To cope in social life, people are advised to be guided by the solicitous attitude of prihatin, to have the wisdom to take life seriously. These responses, however, are personal affairs that have little to do with the demands of social life per se. What they underline, though, is the possibility that the individual has to keep society at a distance, to separate himself from it, and to create his own world.

The kebatinan-inspired moral structure of action

Conforming to the mystical idea that life on earth is only a way station on the journey to origin-and-destination, the material aspects of existence receive little or only negative attention in the kebatinan philosophy of life. The earth on which we live, the things we use, and labour per se, are never considered worthy of pursuit. They constitute a material world from which one has to move away. Man should, of course, accept his obligations to his station in life, but he is discouraged from striving for material improvement and amassing riches. The real riches in life are to be found in social harmony and spiritual development.

Mystically and practically, the social hierarchy is seen as a part of the encompassing order. In both, it only makes sense to look for inspiration, protection, and material advance in the more refined, the more exalted realms of existence. Man alone is a nobody, weak and vulnerable. He should, therefore, surrender to higher forces and superior power, adapt himself to circumstances rather than fight them. It is better not to act than to stir up trouble. It is better to be content with little than to strive for more and be ambitious. As a result, the idealized kebatinan attitudes of acceptance, patience, humility, self-knowledge and modesty, become the very qualities a person should possess in social life. The resulting quiet, harmonious order is the proof of this wisdom, and stands as a sign of the blessing of 'God'.

CHAPTER 5

Kebatinan and society

There is little doubt that mysticism has occupied a place of pride in Javanese culture for a very long time. Claims, however, that its practice was popular long before Hindu-Buddhist ideas reached the island — such as maintained by certain kejawèn people proud of their heritage — are impossible to substantiate. Besides, what mysticism would have amounted to in those remote days would be very difficult to retrace, because we have very little information about early Javanese society. When polities begin to organize according to Indic ideas (hierarchically, under the sway of kings) evidence of the importance of religious establishments and of mystical ideas that promote the ruler's legitimacy, become irrefutable.

With the advent of Islam, and its social organization, things, including mysticism, must have changed, adapting themselves to and being shaped by new circumstances. This is, for instance, apparent in the abundance of Arabic stems — lair, batin, sujud, tarékat — used to describe mystical endeavour. And then, even during the short period under consideration, we note further changes, such as the move away from magical practice, the tendency towards monotheism, and in the relationship between recognized religions and Javanism. Put differently, there is obviously a relationship between the ever-changing shape of society and its cultural products. Thus, while yesterday's thinking still exercises its hold on the life of today, present practice also moulds such thinking to make it relevant rather than old-fashioned.

Kebatinan mysticism, as we know it now, is clearly the product of late colonial society as it existed in the principalities, or sultanates, of South-Central Java. To understand its situation, we need to go down into history. Up to around the twelfth century, powerful, temple-building kingdoms flourished, roughly in the same area that later became known as the *Vorstenlanden*, or said principalities. These so-called Hindu-Buddhist states were clearly heir to Indic civilization and used Sanskrit as the official language of politics and religion. Religion and politics appeared as fused in kingship and the practice of statecraft. The mobilization of magical and religious potency went hand in hand with the practical call to arms of troops, and the rallying of vast masses of labourers. When such kingdoms were not engaged in the politics of forging strategic alliances, they were often at war with each other. In this way, the thriving civilization of South-Central Java somehow self-destructed.

From this time on, the political centre of gravity was to be found in East Java; it is fondly remembered as the great Hindu-Buddhist realm of Majapahit. In those days, we note a shift from Sanskrit to what is called Middle Javanese, in which the vernacular becomes dominant, at the same time as the building of great religious monuments declines. Majapahit was an outward-oriented polity, seaborne trade being one of its economic mainstays. To protect its commerce, or just fired by the imperialistic drive, the kingdom was, for a while, able to impose its sway over vast tracts of maritime Southeast Asia. This fact is still celebrated in current Indonesian historiography, which declares Majapahit to be the predecessor state of the present united archipelagic Republic.

Be that as it may, the commercially strategic location on the routes between China and India attracted traders and others from these countries, and Indic influence was able to firmly establish itself in vast parts of the region — as in Java. By the end of the thirteenth century, and by the same logic of trade, Muslim merchants, and others, had reached the area. They stand at the beginning of the Islamicization process that still continues until this day. In the fifteenth, Islamic kingdoms appear to have had a hold on Java's western and northern coastal lands; Majapahit's days are numbered. When it was finally overrun, sometime between the 1470s and the 1520s, the royal retainer Sabdopalon — often held to be an avatar of Semar — is said to have predicted the resurgence of Hindu-Buddhist culture 'after five hundred years'.

The resulting power vacuum made for unsettled political conditions. It was only in the beginning of the seventeenth century that a powerful kingdom, Mataram, held sway over most of Java again. Meanwhile the Dutch East-India Company, the VOC, had arrived, and the stage was set for the contention between it and the Javanese kings. Sultan Agung (r.1613–46) attacked newly established Batavia twice, but to no avail. He distrusted seaborne commerce, and the merchants' independence and individualism. He ravaged the trading centres on the north coast, bringing Javanese shipping to an end. From his title, sultan, it is clear that the ruler accepted at least the paraphernalia of Islam. Under his descendant, Amangkurat I (r.1646–77), the uneasiness of the coexistence of the new religion and the remnants of the old culture of state is born out by the butchering of thousands of ulemas. Meanwhile, though, the VOC had firmly established its position, and was on its way to become the dominant power on the island of Java.

Rivalries in the Javanese realm proper, combined with the cunning of divide-and-rule politics, resulted in the gradual demise of the kingdom. By the middle of the eighteenth century, Mataram was split into the Sunanate of Solo, or Surakarta, and the Sultanate of Yogyakarta. Later on, two more princes obtained their 'independence', namely, the Mangkunagara of Surakarta, and the Pakualam of Yogya. Gradually, all of them would lose their influence in the outlying territories, until they finally formed the relatively small piece of territory that is now held to be the kejawèn area. In the far-off days of the Company, kejawèn, as we know it today, did not exist. In retrospect, it had, perhaps, just been born as the fruit of the emasculation of the Javanese kings. Through their manipulation by the Dutch, they had become puppets. When, early in the nineteenth century, Java became a colony of the Kingdom of the Netherlands, the princes had been firmly brought into line with the colonial administration. The modicum of self-rulership that was conceded to them resulted in the paraphernalia, in the folklore of kingship. They became masters of ceremonies presiding over a cultural spectacle.

Having almost no political potential, court life became a purpose in itself. The confrontation with the Dutch 'other' necessitated the definition of a Javanese identity. By the second half of the nineteenth century, rarified, orientalized Javanese came into being. According to the Mangkunagara IV (r.1853–81), the land of Java was in the possession of sublime knowledge that, as a religion, inspired its rulers. Rulership had become culture. Vis-à-vis westerners, Javanese became spiritual, mystical, wise. Materialism and technology were set in opposition to sensitivity, refinement, and esoterism.

The discovery of the mysterious Orient, and the emergence and efflorescence of theosophy, have much to do with each other. Europeans were longing for spiritual renewal and the magic of mystery.

The numinous was 'in'. At the same time, certain court-affiliated Javanese discovered their newly forged 'heritage' of wisdom and mysticism in Mangkunagara IV's didactic poem *Wédhatama (Superior Wisdom)*. Javanese and Europeans found each other in the Theosophical Society; in the *Kawruh Beja (Science of Happiness)* of the prince-mystic Ki Ageng Soerjomentaram; in the study of Javanology. And thus, in the same period that the dissemination of western ideas — Marxism, socialism, humanism and nationalism — induced the opening up to a new world and the National Awakening, others were irresistably attracted to spiritualism. The founding fathers of three of the now-thriving sects — Pangestu, Subud and Sumarah — all received their revelations in the twenties and thirties. By recording them, they placed kebatinan mysticism as we know it today on a firm footing.

The interesting contradiction of late colonial society is contained in its awakening to the dynamism of the modern world, and in its celebration of eternal truth. Perhaps this contradiction is indigenous to humanity: when things start moving, and certainty decreases, the need for identity and conviction presents itself. Thus, at the same time that secular nationalism was discovered, others responded to modernity by underlining their Islamic identity, and others still became more consciously Javanese. This Javanist impulse was closely related to the palace, the *kraton*. This is not to say that all cultural kings were personally deeply involved in mysticism, or convinced of the part they played as guardians of 'tradition'. Yet, they were there, and around their persons a highly elaborated and refined culture of the court had developed ever since they had been domesticated. As pillars of colonial rule, they were part of the administrative set-up of their own territories, and of the colony as a whole.

Court society implies nobility, and there was no shortage of royal offspring descending from queens, consorts, concubines and other female talent. This, in itself, readily implied a system of fine gradations of rank, and thus titles, and the related linguistic etiquette. Besides this nobility, there were the 'younger brothers of the king', that is the administrators, functionaries, civil servants, scribes, and teachers — normally recruited from the commoners — who were known as *priyayi*. These, too, earned their ranks and titles. Together, these groups constituted court society, far removed from the ordinary, coarse people.

Highly status-conscious, keen on privilege and distinction, they were also the group which profited from modern education: the colony needed trained administrators and literate clerks.

Needless to say, this hierarchy constituted the backbone of court society. With the king — the mystical companion of the Queen of the Southern Ocean — at its apex, and secluded in a palace full of potent paraphernalia, this hierarchy reckoned rank and status in terms of distance from the ruler. In this sense, it was a highly personalized society where people were known, and somehow equated, with the position they held in the hierarchy. To move upwards, feigning and flattery, intrigue and connivance were as much a means as plain merit and devotion to duty. It stimulated, on the positive side, the remarkable elaboration of etiquette, of good form, and the ideas of order and harmony. These, as such, became the hallmark of the refined priyayi gentleman. Mastery of self and manners was complemented by the moral advice to be acceptant of one's position, to be grateful because of it, and to cultivate humility, patience, modesty, and suchlike.

However wise such advice might be, it stands in some opposition to a highly stratified arrangement, where persons are seen in terms of positions and ranks, where they identify with status while hoping to improve it. Status consciousness implies status competition, pride, and sensitivity to honour. Status identity implies a masquerade. Together these make for a wooden society of two-dimensional characters, where motives are dissembled, and where things are — by convention — taken at face value. Yet — and everybody knows — there is much more to life than appearances. Perhaps there is even an escape from wooden orderedness, where things are only good when they are in place.

Mysticism readily became a priyayi pursuit — and for many reasons. The dictates of society required self-discipline and mastery. The cultivation of a strong batin could be nothing but very helpful to this end. A quiet, equanimous inner life is definitely conducive to entertaining acquiescence, humbleness, self-effacement, and similar qualities. These easily underline the nothingness of people, and the fact that all is in God's hands. The greatest attraction of the mystical practice was — probably — that it frees from social demands, that it creates a world all its own which seemingly even contains truth far superior to that which ordinary life can offer. In that sphere, the personal experience is validated, and in spite of nothingness, ego becomes important. The frustrations of human existence do not seem to matter any longer. Kebatinan individualizes, and creates distance.

So, whereas the lowest stage of the mystical path still emphasizes ritual, and so, for the priyayi, the following of the requirements of a wooden order, his 'honouring of parents, elder brother, guru and king' is surpassed by attaining inner freedom. Because he is able to separate the inner from the outer realm, this does not make him an iconoclast. Let the outer realm be; let it be ordered by practising values, by giving shape to culture, by maintaining harmony. What matters is inner development and, if he advances further, when he really gets to the goal, he will shine like a beacon in this world.

Practically, and mystically, social conditions seem to follow from personal endeavour, whether from values or from laku, the following of the ascetic path. These create social equilibrium, an idealized stasis where things are in place, and where persons have become positions. Together they form a totality, a oneness of being presided over by the dynast, by the 'master of ceremonies'. This tangible image of society reflects its being in step with ideal cosmological conditions; it is coordinated, so to speak, with truth and high purpose.

It seems unlikely that such a social arrangement ever really existed and, as we have seen, late colonial society was in considerable flux. Things had been set in motion, and much in court society, too, was changing. Yet the ideal of stasis — of unity, harmony, being in step, and equilibrium — became superattractive in reaction to modernity and the emotion-laden process of national awakening. Javanism, containing that sublime knowledge — the religion of the ruler — held the key to achieving equanimity of the inner being and social balance. This development towards the self-orientalization of palace-oriented society resulted in it becoming a holy heirloom, a pusaka in itself. It became the noble heritage from which people could draw their inspiration when change gained momentum; when society, because of war, revolution, political contention, and religious strife, appeared to be ever more in turmoil rather than in flux.

Summary

For us, it is good to realize ourselves the origins of modern mysticism, and to be conscious that it evolved in the context of late colonial society — itself a time of rapid change — when Javanese kingship was politically powerless, yet culturally productive. Whereas many kebatinan adepts claim their practice to predate even the period of Indic influence, the shape and world of thought it inhabits at present is clearly the result of rather recent occurrences. These days, however, it is often held to contain the essence of Javaneseness, even of Indonesianness. It is glorified, by some, as timeless heritage, as self-validating tradition. It is a climate of thought that informs the political-cultural practice of the present.

CHAPTER 6

Summarizing the Javanist world view

Unity of existence

Seen in a cosmological perspective, all belongs together, not in a haphazard way, but as a regulated whole that is subject to preordination rather than volition. This predetermination is known as the principle of necessity. The outcome of preordination, *kebeneran*, translates as truth, manifestation, and coincidence. This cosmology is often illustrated by the shadow play mythology that contains the Javanese elaboration of the *Mahabharata* cycle, with the *Bhagavad Gita* at its core.

This vision of man recognizes that humans are part of the cosmos, but in a special way. First of all, they can choose; they have free will. Their choices may be uneducated (stupid, emotional, immoral) or educated (wise, conscious, moral). Secondly, humans are considered to consist of two parts, a phenomenal lair and an inner batin. To the phenomenal part belong the five senses, and the capacity for rational thought. The inner part is secretive, constituting the line to one's origin, and containing a spark of Life itself; to it belongs the sixth sense, the intuitive inner feeling, known as rasa, which is the instrument for deep insight and revelation.

Social relationships should, like cosmic ones, be well-ordered and combine in a harmonious totality. According to the Javanese view of society, such relationships are hierarchically organized, people being the occupants of certain status positions that relate to each other in morally unequal ways. This order of society is a part of the total cosmic order.

From these considerations follows the kejawèn ethic, such as the imperative to seek budaya ('culture': knowledge and wisdom). With that, one will know one's place in society and in all-encompassing Life; one will also know the ethic and task that belong to one's place. People should live attuned to it all. In their phenomenal existence they should respect the order of society, honour elders and superiors, and be considerate of inferiors by taking 'the measure of oneself'. They should care about harmonious relationships, at least outwardly so, and thus avoid all open conflict. To do this requires knowledge and mastery of the self, of drives and emotions. People must cultivate and strengthen their inner self, their batin.

In its widest sense, this cultivation of the inner self is known as kebatinan, or as olah rasa, the training of the inner feeling. A strong batin enables a person not to be perturbed by whatever happens in the phenomenal world, and to be patient. It enables people to accept life as it comes and to adjust to it. It is a training in sensing and feeling, which results in knowing when the right moment to act has arrived; in feeling attuned to cosmic happenings; in attempting to be in step with the Divine Principle, or Life, and eventually in seeking union of the self with origin-and-destination, thus realizing Truth. It is only in this last, mystical, sense that kebatinan has clear religious overtones; as the cultivation of the mind and inner feeling it is the kejawèn way to wisdom and an ethical life.

Whichever the case, to live attuned to what is greater than oneself, be it the order of society or the cosmos, cannot but be moral and wise. Disturbance of this order is immoral and foolish. Since society is part of the totality, respect for its structure may already signify reverence for the system of Life and a way of honouring 'God'. One's moral obligation is to fulfil one's life and position in the world, therefore eschatological speculation and expectations are only weakly developed. Life is really in the here-and-now.

The kejawèn stress on kebatinan leads to a strong self-centredness. In one's batin, one is important; the experience of society, its rules and sufferings, should be accepted, but the real truth is contained in the deep self. A person's moral and ethical task is to cultivate the mind, to seek wisdom, and fulfil one's place in a universe of unequal positions. Harmonious relationships with others guarantee an undisturbed batin/inner life while, at the same time, conflict avoidance, self-centredness, and self-fulfilment foster a great measure of tolerance vis-à-vis other people. In the batin, everybody is potentially free, in spite of a restrictive, hierarchically ordered society.

People who cultivate their batin by way of ascetic exercises may do so for all kinds of secular purposes, such as solicitude, or prihatin, about the immediate course in life, or the future of the children. It is an expression of taking life seriously, of taking care. Some people practise kebatinan for a religious purpose, such as mysticism. Because there is no dividing line between the secular and the sacred in kejawèn thinking, it is hard to say whether the kejawèn way of life is in itself an expression of *agami jawi*, as Javanese religion is called.[5] This much is certain, the kejawèn philosophy of life fosters a religious attitude, mysticism, and self-centredness, at the same time as it devalues expectations about the afterlife, institutionalized religion, and the fulfilment of religious obligations.

Rasa

Naturally, the kebatinan view of life allows for the analysis of reality at a number of levels. This can be seen above, for instance, in the division of a phenomenal lair world from its inner batin core, and also in the recognition of a world of rationality and a less volitional world of mystery. All these seem to combine at the level of rasa. Mystically and practically, rasa may be described as the intuitive inner feeling that everyone possesses. Some people, though, have a more refined rasa than others, and are thus sensitive to things that escape the attention of the less finely tuned.

In its most common sense, rasa means taste and feeling, such as the taste of rice or the feeling of sickness; it means the physical sense of touch, as well. It also stands for the fundamental nature of a substance, or its true being. It is the personal instrument leading to true insight, being one's essence and one's part in The Essence. Often it is used interchangeably with *rahsa* or *rahasya*, meaning secret, hidden, mysterious — and in one of its meanings, semen, it may stand for 'vehicle of life'.

Often Javanese juxtapose rasa and ordinary common sense *(nalar; akal)*, or the instrument for understanding the phenomenal world and

---

5 For a different position, equating Javanism with *Agami Jawi* (Javanese religion), see Koentjaraningrat 1985:316-79. If Javanese religion can be defined by its practices, I suggest that observance of the slametan rituals; *nyadran* (paying respect and prayer to deceased parents — also rulers and religious personalities — at their graves), and periodical *sesajèn* (offerings) to spirits, may be considered as defining characteristics.

its mundane affairs. Such rationality, though, cannot reveal the essence of the phenomenal world; this can only be grasped by the personal intuitive inner feeling. From the kejawèn perspective, real knowledge is both mysterious and subjective; it is personal insight into the true nature of things that cannot be formulated objectively. It is in and from oneself that 'truth' can be grasped through training in intuitive sensitivity. Consequently, the kejawèn quest for knowledge is informed by fascination for mystery, and the elusive knowledge of 'God' is no better than a personal experience. No wonder that there is an absence of dogma and generally accepted theology. These cannot be part of the intrinsically open-ended idea of knowledge.

It comes, therefore, as no surprise that Javanese teachings should be full of symbolism and esoteric knowledge that stimulate fantasy and reflection. Such teachings are also contained in the old shadow theatre mythology that is inspired by the *Mahabharata*, in which life on earth appears to be a mere reflection, a shadow of higher truth and realities. The illumination so attained can only be intuited rather than reasoned. This contrasts sharply with the themes of certain modern shadow plays that have, for instance, the birth of Christ as their subject.

This Catholic innovation attempts to communicate a message through scenes that spell out an explicit orthodoxy, which by its nature cannot stimulate a variety of interpretations, nor foster free association around its symbolism; it thus does not stimulate the predilection for mystery. The interpretation of the shadowy world of mythology should be deeply subjective, transcending historical truth while stimulating the personal imagination. Somehow, things are not as interesting, nor as much fun, if they are plain and clear.

This contrast between the interest in objective versus subjective knowledge is also borne out by the experience of a European Catholic priest working as a long-time missionary in Java. He told me about his frustrations, while teaching at seminary, in explaining the importance of the historicity of Christ. The fact that Jesus had been there, that he was a historical person who had really been on earth, was the keystone of his faith. Yet he complained that his Javanese students were not impressed by such facts, being far more interested in the mystical significance of Christ. I think that no Christian Javanese will take it as a mere coincidence that the priest's name was Thomas.

Order

The unity of existence is essentially mysterious, yet it constitutes a regulated order of which life on earth is also an expression, a *wayangan* (shadow), as it were, of higher truth. This unity is subject to cosmic law, that is, the law of necessity or ukum pinesthi, which states that all creation has to run its preordained course. Life, while setting limits to experience, purpose and volition, is also an inescapable — and necessary — progression for all, without exception. It is an ordered and coordinated whole, which people must accept, and to which they have to adapt themselves.

People, therefore, have the moral duty to respect the order of existence. They should acquiesce in life as it comes, while cultivating a state of inner peace and emotional calm. Impulsive actions, or yielding to one's lusts and desires, giving free rein to passions, are reprehensible because they upset personal, social and cosmic order. People should thus master themselves, inwardly and outwardly; doing this means shaping life beautifully.

Nrima (accepting) means knowing one's place, means trust in fate and gratefulness to 'God', because there is satisfaction in fulfilling one's lot in the consciousness that all has been destined. One should consciously follow the path of destiny from which, anyhow, there is no escaping. This does not mean that a person should not strive to make the best of it, because he can know the results of his lot only by the outcome of his actions. It thus makes sense to be active in shaping life in the consciousness of fulfilling one's task in the great order.

This notion of task, or obligation to station in life, is illustrated by the well-known episode from the *Mahabharata* in which the hero Karno has to face Arjuna. Karno is the half-brother of Arjuna and the other Pendawa — the five brothers who symbolize order, righteousness and justice. In the great war, the Bharata Yuddha, they have to fight their cousins, the Kurawa, who stand for the forces of disorder, passion and desire. It is Karno's lot to serve on the side of the Kurawa, thus facing his half-brothers in battle. After having killed Gathutkaca, Bima's favourite son, he knows that he will have to die at the hands of Arjuna. As a noble warrior, a real kshatriya, he is true to his position in life, to his fate and obligation to his king, fighting valiantly until he is killed. It is his opponent Arjuna who hesitates and wavers, reluctant to accept his duty to kill Karno. Upon turning to his divine counsellor Kresna (Krishna), he is urged to carry out his duty, this wavering being weak and condemnable, because it is his destiny to kill Karno.

While both finally fulfilled their duty in implementing the course of history, to many the real hero is Karno, as he personifies the moral example of a man who follows his duty and destiny without hesitation. His fate is in the hands of 'God', the best he can do is to accept it and shape it beautifully. Such is a true hero; such, also, is a moral man. Life and destiny are ordered in a scheme that is beyond human volition, and in which moral choice means faithfulness to position and obligation.

The fact that life is subject to cosmic law and part of an inescapable order stimulates fascination with prophecy and projective action. Because the cosmic design has been 'fixed', it may also be known; it remains a matter of discovering its coordinates to know the future. Prediction is thus possible if one has access to the great scheme by way of meditation or mystical practice, magical calculation or knowledge of horoscopy.

For example, when walking the streets of Yogya, one may come across a group of tricycle drivers squatting on the pavement, one of them scribbling figures and lines on the ground. They are busy discussing the meaning of a revealing symbol that has, perhaps, been published in that day's newspaper; they are calculating the outcome of next Saturday's lottery. They are searching for the truth, as it were, for the hidden shape of reality to come. Part of that secret has already been revealed in the published symbol. It is up to them to interpret it and to calculate the number that is predestined, although not yet visible. Theirs is a very utilitarian attempt to discover the as yet unrevealed course of the future.

Events do not happen because of chance, but manifest themselves because of hidden forces that bring about each co-incidence, each kebeneran. A new event is a crossroad, a co-inciding, in which the shadow of inevitability becomes a fact. This notion of causality is at the same time both extremely pragmatic and deeply mystical, giving reason to activity and the endeavour to uncover the structure of events to come. Therefore, people will calculate auspicious days to start a venture, and marriage partners should be matched on the basis of characterological and horoscopical singularities to ensure that they fit. Once the right formula or the right coordinates have been established, action may be initiated in the expectation that it will develop auspiciously, in other words, without causing disturbance of good order.

Sometimes conditions and events may be recognized as threatening and potentially disturbing, in which case they should be constrained by ceremony and ritual. Basically, such constraining, called *ngruwat*, is an attempt to change inauspicious coordinates to orderly ones, to undo the evil spell that hovers over persons who suffer from involuntary states of affliction, who are *sukerta*. Long lists can be drawn of inauspicious birth constellations and other circumstances that attract danger, thus calling for ritual intervention. This demonstrates that the coordinated nature of the unity of existence is two-sided: man plays as much a role in the working of order as any of the other impersonal forces that influence it. Naturally, this idea stimulates the desire to make order transparent. Yet even if momentarily crystal clear, order, much like the knowledge of it, remains shifting and elusive; it thus makes sense to influence its course by ritual and projective action. Whatever the case, the disturbance of good order is basically sinful, as much as it is to upset it by emotion or magical practice. On the other hand, action that is directed at re-establishing order, or its auspicious continuation, is right in itself.

Slametan

The core ritual to sustain, maintain, or promote order is the slametan, a communal religious meal in which neighbours plus some relatives and friends participate. Their purpose is to achieve the state of *slamet*, which Koentjaraningrat once described as 'a state in which events run their fixed course smoothly and nothing untoward happens to anyone'.

Such invocations are held at all of life's important occasions, and at communal celebrations, in order to ensure undisturbed continuity. They are also staged when well-being and equilibrium have been affected. In theory, all participants enjoy the same ritual status, each person contributing equally to the spiritual power of the event. The slametan, therefore, serves to demonstrate the harmonious community known as rukun, which is the prerequisite for effectively evoking the blessing of gods, spirits and ancestors.

Slametan demonstrate the desire to be safe in an unruly world. They do not aim at a better life, now or in the future, but rather at the maintenance of order and the constraining of danger. It also appears, however, that humans play an active role in maintaining this order and can influence its course, well-ordered social relationships being a means to and a condition for promoting the state of slamet.

Continuance of life

The social pattern is often thought to be the microcosm of the order of Life, the basic model of which is the family. It is the normal task of every adult to seek the continuation of life within Life, to marry and have offspring. Parents, having been born before their children, are in a superior moral position and have the duty to care for their children from before birth until they are married, when the latter take over the task of continuing the lineage.

Apart from being givers of life and moral superiors, progenitors are also an important source of blessing for their children. At the end of Ramadan, the month of fasting, children should present themselves before their parents, kneel in front of them, ask their forgiveness, and seek their blessing. Then, after their parents' deaths, children should visit and take care of the graves. There, the *jasa* (merit) of parents is thought to flow out, as a protective magical force, to their descendants who will pray to their souls and seek guidance.

Parents, as representatives of life and its order, are entitled to the highest honour, and children should *ngabekti*, pay homage and service to them as a quasi-religious act. To respect their moral superiority is honouring Life, which is often further elaborated in the notion that honouring superiors is equivalent to revering 'God'. This notion very clearly demonstrates the hierarchical concept of order, in which the inferior should respect all those who are closer to the sources of life, moral wisdom and power. To live in harmony with them is moral behaviour per se.

In consequence, it is sinful not to honour one's parents, not to accept their advice, or to hurt their feelings. Such behaviour is thought to establish a serious infraction of the moral order and will invoke automatic supernatural retribution, known as *walat*. This powerful sanction — especially relevant to understand the inviolable nature of parents — is one of the best safeguards for maintaining hierarchy and order.

Bonds beyond those with parents are not generally thought to be protected by supernatural sanction, but highlight the importance of keeping working relationships smooth. After all, people are mutually dependent, which is also illustrated by the slametan. In order for a slametan to be ritually effective, neighbours must participate too, even if the occasion has been staged to ensure one's personal well-being. Therefore, it is imperative to cultivate each other's goodwill by observing rukun, respecting sensitivities, being tolerant, and contributing to common rituals, such as communal slametan and burials.

Kebatinan

However imperative all the aforementioned beliefs and rituals are, nonetheless the vital core of kejawèn is thought to be in kebatinan, by which is meant the cultivation of the inner being and secret self. It is that deep self that really constitutes the quintessence of all-encompassing Life. In many characteristic similes, the experience of life itself is described as a journey from origin to destination, from conception to reabsorption with the All. In the kebatinan view, this self-training should move from the outside to the inside, from the mastery of the lair to the cultivation of the batin, from becoming fully aware of one's social surroundings to becoming sensitized to the presence of Life and the realization of it in one's inner being; it means coordinating the self with higher truth until one fuses with it.

The idea that treading the mystical path is a journey on the way to truth and self-realization, is vividly illustrated by the well-known *Dewa Ruci* narrative that relates Bima's quest to discover the secret of life. Soon after setting out, he is led astray by false advice, while later on meeting with all kinds of dreadful dangers and the trials of the wilderness. Then, arriving on the beach, he is told to find the secret — the water of life — hidden in the profundity of the ocean. When, after overcoming further challenges, he finally reaches the depths of the great sea, he meets with a miniature double of himself, Dewa Ruci, who instructs Bima to enter through its ear in order to find the secret of life. This story symbolizes the lonely mystical quest of man who has to overcome himself before he is led to the source of truth and wisdom, that he can only discover by descending into the depth of his own inner being. After conquering his passions and delusions, it is there that 'God' can be found, the unity of existence ultimately being realized in one's deep self.

The essence of modern kebatinan lies in self-mastery and sensitivity. It centres on the self, in the hope of realizing the perfection of life, irrespective of one's social surroundings. It is an ethical way to wisdom and balance that need not be religiously expressed, although it always entails the cultivation of the batin and the exercise of refining one's intuitive inner feeling, or rasa, to sense the true dimensions of existence. To follow this path, one should be trained: 'When young and ignorant, father is needed as the first teacher. Later, one seeks a master who knows more, or other things, then on to others, until ultimately Bathara Guru ("God") takes over'. At this last stage, of course, each person is alone, the discrete individual becoming the centre of insight in life, and its order.

In the mystical perspective, this thinking is expressed in the idea of achieving unity between servant and Master *(manunggaling kawula-Gusti)*. To reach this, one has to overcome the fetters that tie each individual to phenomenal existence, such as passions and worldly rationality, which lead only to a delusive perception of truth. In the same vein, the mystical adept should be free from egoistic motives, from pamrih, when training to be attuned to Life. Social existence with its ritual exigencies, including the ceremonies of formal religion, become mere outward requirements — useful, perhaps, as disciplinary practice. It remains remote from the profound experience that opens the really important dimension of life, giving access to truth, guidance and revelation from 'God'.

The practice of kebatinan is an individual-centred endeavour that places the deep self, the 'true I' *(Aku; ingsun sejati)*, at the very centre of all evaluation. It is the development of rasa that becomes the measuring rod of inner growth. The ultimate stage is to realize the conviction that one lives in step with Life, and has access to truth in a direct, unmediated way, drawing power from 'God' while, at the same time, being independent from sources of truth outside the deep self. The practice of kebatinan may thus be seen as a personal pursuit toward self-realization by building up strong inner resources so that finally one is guided by wahyu (divine revelation) and kasunyatan (ultimate truth). Its basis is the conviction that individual life and inner feeling constitute the valid centre of all experience, and the conclusive empirical, self-validating testing ground for truth.

CHAPTER 7

Resurgence of kejawèn: Indonesian ideology

To say that culture is process is little better than a platitude. Yet, when we note that Indonesian culture is 'in process', we may hit upon a more meaningful characteristic. Indonesian culture is in the making — and nobody really knows what it is. Indonesia is a young state, and this name for the country became current in nationalist circles as recently as the 1920s. In other words, what Indonesia, and being Indonesian, are supposed to mean, needs to be constructed; and this endeavour is still going on.

The need for unity in diversity was recognized early on, as Indonesia is the successor state of a colonial empire that brought countless nations, cultures and languages under one sway, and which extended for five-thousand kilometres along the equator — one eighth of the circumference of the globe! As early as 1928, the nationalists had given impetus to this necessary ideal: the domain of the Netherlands Indies was said to constitute one country, inhabited by one nation, speaking one language. From before independence and on into the present, the shaping of this ideal has preoccupied nationalists and government alike.

There is little 'natural' about the unity of the far-flung archipelago. According to the founding fathers, it was the deep-seated desire to be together, a wish born from the suffering of colonization, that bound the various populations together. What they shared, what they had in common, had largely to be invented. Indonesian culture would consist of the best each local ethnic group had to offer, which means that it was thought to be an amalgam, a composition. Yet, there must also be an underlying commonality. It was Sukarno's genius to formulate the Pancasila, and to make people believe that it was its five principles they shared — since time immemorial.

However attractive this unitary ideology might be, not all were convinced. Some people aspired to an Islamic state, and soon the opposition between Muslim orthodoxy, and proponents of the separation of the worldly from the religious, became apparent. Within the Revolution, certain groups went their own way, and fought the others. In its aftermath, several regions tried to break away, to impose their will, or to establish themselves on an Islamic basis. The extreme violence of 1965–66 demonstrated that unity could, by no means, be taken for granted.

It is, therefore, little cause for wonder that the New Order dispensation has made *persatuan dan kesatuan* (unity and integrity) its all-overriding fetish. This preoccupation is nothing intrinsically Javanese; all states strive for and defend their integrity. To do this, the Indonesian regime incessantly stresses the importance of the Pancasila while claiming that it gives shape to its principles, and to those contained in the Constitution of 1945, in a pure and consistent manner. Combined these constitute the mandate and the foundation of the New Order, the guardian of the nation.

If there is any substance to Indonesian culture, it must indeed be the Pancasila. Or is it Javanese? Somehow, the use of the Pancasila seems to suffer from an obsession that is more than just defending national integrity or the professed national emblem of 'Unity in Diversity'. It smells of a fear of diversity, which is, of course, nothing strange in the military-coloured culture of the incumbent government. Nowadays, all social organizations must acknowledge the Pancasila as their ideological basis. Pancasila takes precedence over religion and political ideology. Diversity must be overcome, just like the mystic must overcome the confusion induced by his senses, until he fuses with the One.

Through the years, the Pancasila has been understood in a great variety of ways. It spawned — and continues to originate — a vast literature, mainly of Javanistic reflections, that parallels the production of religious dogmatic, philosophical and moralistic treatises. As such, it is a sacred heirloom, a pusaka; it is a protective talisman, an *azimat*; it is sacred in itself, it is *sakti*; it is the origin and destination of Indonesian society; it is the compass of the people; it is the source of all law; it is the guarantor of the oneness and integrity of the country; it is the dearest possession of the nation. According to Sukarno, the five principles can be conflated into one, gotong-royong (mutual assistance); others reduce them to Ketuhanan, worship of God Almighty. It seems as if the Pancasila has acquired mystical qualities; it appears as a mystical stream by itself.

Javanization

Since the Javanese constitute by far the largest ethnic group, and since they cultivate a high awareness of culture, of their civilization, it does not come as a surprise that their influence on what passes for the Indonesian climate of thought is strong, not to say dominant. This is most apparent under current conditions, but nothing new as such. As we have seen, during the old regime the interpretation of the holy number 17–8–1945 flourished. At that time, we could also witness the beginning of Pancasila literature; and Sukarno's sloganeering made the impression of trying to master the polity by imposing powerful mantras.

It cannot be denied, though, that the flood of mantra-like formulae[6] has accelerated in the New Order period. At its very birth stands the auspicious word *Supersemar*, invoking, as such, the blessing of the God of Java, the progenitor of the Javanese race, the idea *super* even alluding to his full divine manisfestation Ismaya, elder brother of Shiva. And, as everybody familiar with the shadow theatre knows, Semar only backs winners. The word itself, Supersemar, is nothing but the acronym of *surat perintah sebelas Maret*, or President Sukarno's putative command to General Soeharto to bring order to the country. This command happened to be given on the eleventh day of March. It is a pity that nobody has seen this document ever since; it was filed somewhere, and has not been retrieved to this day — but this is a minor matter. The important thing is that a highly auspicious formula inaugurated the New Order, and with the Javanese sense for coordination and co-incidence, Supersemar is a true kebeneran — no accidental occurrence. And as with the older Javanese pastime of constructing somewhat esoteric chronograms, it is difficult to believe that the said mantra-like invocation would be the product of chance.

6 For instance, Second National Awakening; IPTEK (Science and Technology); *semangat* (spirit); *tinggal landas* (take-off); Pancasila man; *UUD 45* (Constitution of 1945); *Pembangunan* (Development); Trilogi Pembangunan; *menyukseskan* (to make things a success); *Pemilu* (elections); *Pesta Demokrasi* (the running-up period to the five-yearly elections); Pancasila; *Pelita* (Five-Year Plan); Long Term Development Plan; *warisan kebudayaan* (cultural heritage); *upacara* ('traditional' ceremony); *KB* (family planning); *serasi, selaras, seimbang* (harmonious); *Wawasan Nusantara*; *Ipoleksosbudhankam* (the mystical unity of Wawasan Nusantara); *monodualistik*.

In the subsequent course of stabilization, Pancasila and Constitution of 1945 became full-blown and unchangeable sacred heirlooms. They became holy formula protecting the nation. They were reified, turned into objects the possession of which legitimated the regime and blessed the course it sailed. They became like a wahyu, a divine mandate. After all, when in the possession of the right mantras, a ruler can do no wrong. It is because of the Pancasila that the nation exists; it is because of its quality of holy heirloom that the nation did not disintegrate. The God-given scheme — Necessity — has been revealed. It is to mould the world of Indonesia and, above all, preserve its unity and integrity.

Origin-and-destination are known. These merely need to be given shape. Thus, obdurate reality needs to be pushed, forced, and stimulated; it needs to be worked on. This activity is called Development. It has two aspects: an outward, material one, and an inward, spiritual one. This last, this inner component of the national effort is to create the Pancasila personality, the Complete Indonesian Man, inhabiting a harmonious, stable, yet dynamic society. Always guided by the common interest, his ego-drives effaced, he is active for the benefit of all, making the country a better and more beautiful place. *Sepi ing pamrih, ramé ing gawé. Mamayu hayuning buwana!*

To me, the surfacing of such patterns of thought — perhaps purely ideological, yet powerfully promoted — is a sign of the Javanization of Indonesian culture. To others, Javanization may mean different things. Some point to the transmigration of Javanese peasants to the poorly populated Outer Islands. In itself, this notion of Outer Indonesia is revealing: Java is the centre, the heart, the batin of the country, and shouldn't the batin dominate the outer aspects? Be this as it may, the spread of Javanese populations all over the country, in a way, Javanizes it. Needless to say, this does not necessarily equate with the extension of happiness. In a similar vein, the fact that most officers (some eighty-nine per cent of them) and most high-ranking civil servants and provincial governors hail from Java, makes some people talk about Javanese imperialism. To them, the Javanese are the new masters — they define what is Indonesia and Indonesian.

To others still, including many modern-minded Javanese themselves, *jawanisasi* refers to ways of behaviour they most often denounce. They will draw attention to the tendencies to be arrogant, to be obsessed by self, position, and power, and to show these off. They describe it as neofeudalism and *neopriyayi-isme*. Some of them use the word *Mataramisasi* (to demonstrate power and pull rank) in obvious reference to the ways of court society of yore. They find the manners of the *nouveaux riches* distasteful, and are critical of their flaunting their wealth — not only unashamedly, but to create prestige. Almost every day, newspapers carry pictures of society weddings staged in expensive hotels that meticulously follow a protocol that is thought to imitate the rites of the nobility. Especially since money came in in a great way in the early 1970s, such display spending has become fashionable, and has been dressed up in a 'Javanese' cloak. Meanwhile, many people hold such ceremonies, which include Javanese-style dress and gamelan music, to be national, to be Indonesian.

Javanization is also apparent in the promotion of the Pancasila as official ideology. Since 1978, the state has been very active in spreading its interpretation of the five principles. Together, these were elevated to become the world view of the Indonesian nation, or the philosophy of life that is to give direction to country, people, and state. From this thinking, it followed almost logically to declare, in 1985, the Pancasila to be the unique basis of all organized life in the land: Pancasila supersedes particular religions and political ideologies. All people are expected to become Pancasilaists. All will be united in one stream of thinking. Together they will form the Pancasila society, peopled by whole Indonesian human beings.

To shape this ambition, the state started propagating its vision. At school, the Pancasila course became known as moral education — a compulsory subject in all grades up to university. The older generation, too, need to be moulded in this mentality. For their benefit, a massive national effort was initiated, known as the Four P's, the *P4*. These P's stand for *Pedoman Penghayatan dan Pengamalan Pancasila*, or the Directive for the Full Understanding and Practice of the Pancasila. All people working for the state must attend the courses offered under this programme, and need to show up time and again for refresher courses. Other people, too, are expected to have their mentality upgraded by following suit. To make the exercise more 'attractive', it has been given a deeper name. After all, things that are plain and clear are far less interesting. And thus the course was rebaptized as *Ekaprasetia Pancakarsa*.

> Ekaprasetia Pancakarsa derives from Sanskrit. Literally, 'eka' means one, or one and only; 'prasetia' means promise, or resolve; 'panca' means five; and 'karsa' means strong desire. Ekaprasetia Pancakarsa thus means the oneness of resolve to implement the five wishes ... these five strong wishes are the desire to cause the five moral principles of the Pancasila to materialize. It is called the oneness of resolve because this will is very strong and unshakable (*Bahan Penataran* 1990:27).

The tendency to cloak things in mystery — or at least, in language that is difficult to understand — is also apparent when plain Javanese is used to explain Pancasila leadership. Somehow, Indonesian does not do — or perhaps, this language does not allow for the same scope of interpretation and mystification as Javanese. A Pancasila leader, therefore, is endowed with the qualities of *ing ngarso sung tulodo*, to be so exemplary that people will follow out of conviction; *ing madya mangun karso*, to stimulate his clients' will and creativity; and *tut wuri handayani*, to foster their initiative and responsibility. A leader must thus have the qualities of a guardian, or protector (*pengasuh*, which is plain Indonesian again), who stimulates, leads and guides the ones he has to bring up *(asuhannya)* (*Bahan Penataran* 1990:33). A Pancasila leader therefore equates with the ideal father.

There is no doubt that the state sees itself in a father-like position vis-à-vis the population at large, which is also clear from the manipulation of language in the course materials. By declaring the leader to be a pengasuh ('nurse'; 'guardian'), the people are pushed into the position of children whose initiative should be curbed. Besides, the original educational idea behind the Javanese formula aims at stimulating students: a teacher should 'lead by example in the front, inspire in their midst, and encourage from behind'.

From these various examples, it may be clear that the idea of Javanization is far from unequivocal. To many Javanese, who cultivate a high awareness of what they hold to be their noble heritage, New Order jawanisasi is an insult to Javanese civilization. They would point out the reversal of meaning in the interpretation of leadership. According to them, Javanese ideas, as they surfaced early on this century, unambiguously demonstrate that the people of South-Central Java were perfectly capable of finding their own accommodation with modern times. In education, initiative should be fostered. In imagining, then constructing the nation, they opened out to the world of Indonesia. There were moves to do away with speech levels and hierarchy. People became more conscious, not only of things cultural, but also of change and modernity, of which they were not afraid at all. As a result, they are not happy with neofeudalistic developments, with Mataramization and imitations of royal wedding ritual. Maybe they are not pleased either when reminded of the 'Javanese' inspiration of Pancasila indoctrination.

Be this as it may, at school there is no escape from the doctrine of the state. Since 1994, the course concerned is called 'Pancasila and Civics Education'. It is mandatory at all levels, over twelve years. The teaching of the other social subjects, such as history, sociology, and anthropology, follows the same model. The Pancasila is an old heritage, uniting the Indonesians past and present. All social studies, therefore, must be interpreted in that mould; in other words, state propaganda permeates the teaching of history, sociology and anthropology. It is not our purpose here to picture the image of society that the social studies curriculum evokes; reflections on this image will be the subject of a separate monograph. What will be examined is the state ideology as it is presented in the upper grades of high school. When studying these materials, I was struck by the parallelism they demonstrate with mystical patterns of thought. This convergence, and the type of society they belong to, will be pointed out and commented upon later. Then we may also raise the question as to whether the resulting type of jawanisasi is not somewhat out of step with the world the students live in.

Indoctrination

In Indonesia, indoctrination is big business. Individuals must be subjugated by the state. They are seen as subjects. Citizens, autonomous persons, individualists, all such people pose a danger to a quiet and orderly society. Civil servants must be 'monoloyal', meaning that they serve the state hand and foot, identify with it unwaveringly, vote for its party.

They must be members of *Korpri*, the official organization of the corps of Indonesian state functionaries. To be member of a trade union on the side would go against the principle of *monoloyalitas* (besides, trade unions are illegal). Their wives must be members of Dharma Wanita, and will be convinced that their mission in life, their darma, is to be one-hundred per cent loyal to their husbands whose primary loyalty is to the state. Needless to say, the same goes for soldiers, perhaps even more stringently so, and their wives are supposed to play second — or rather, penultimate — fiddle, as members of the Dharma Pertiwi.

The point here is the massive state effort to organize and legitimize relationships. Among the people most directly under its power, the relation to their patron must be made absolutely clear. And wives should know their place, too. They serve. They are devoted spouses, economical housekeepers, dedicated mothers, real *Ibu*. It is these very people who are the first to be exposed to the P4 programme — and its refresher courses. The popular soap operas national television releases reinforce the messages concerned, and spread them around a much wider public. The objective is to make people conceive of themselves in certain ways — and to convince them of the vision the state ideologues present them with, such as the necessity of Development, the New Order's ushering in a period of 'take-off', a Second National Awakening, and suchlike. The nation is on its way to fulfil the Pancasila society. Its people will be Pancasila men. Communism, liberalism, western-style democracy, free-for-all capitalism, individualism — such are the enemies of 'our' ideals. By enforcing stability and security, through vigilance-without-end, we can suppress such subversion.

Over years, systematic indoctrination has its effects — were it only to dull the spirit, to instil military-style patterns of thought, to compartmentalize life in a moralistic and a practical sector, and to be wary of free speech. To reach these objectives, school provides one of the most powerful tools. Of necessity, indoctrination is a repetitious procedure: the same subject matter is reiterated over and over again to become part of the target's mental make-up. Perhaps it just causes boredom. Perhaps it convinces students that all of it is a sham, that there is an awesome gap between official knowledge and everyday life, that what the government preaches has little to do with what it practises. These questions will not concern us here. Rather, I shall excerpt and paraphrase the course material of the four highest grades of high school, yet attempt to avoid the built-in overlap. This material will be commented on later.

'Pancasila and Civics Education'

From the first until the last grade, the course has been divided into chapters that are presented under snappy headings, such as 'Obedience', 'Concord', 'Sovereignty', 'Obsequiousness', 'Unity', which often have little to do with the matters discussed. Under 'Obedience', the first chapter for the ninth grade offers some interesting thinking about religion. There, the thesis is advanced that the quality of faith in and devotion to God conditions how much people will obey His will and be benevolent to each other. Besides, religious teachings regulate human life completely, and result in most beneficial and useful conditions for social, national, and state life. Religion stresses honesty, hard work, good deeds, and aversion to sin. And thus it is good for all of us to promote the quality of religious life, through devoted worship, social harmony, and service to nation and state. Devotion stimulates peaceful conditions, and participation in national development. After all, such participation is a valuable aspect of worship.

Faithful obedience to and worship of God is reflected in the three dimensions of religious practice, namely, the relationship with God, with fellow men, and with the environment. People praise the Lord, follow His commands, and refrain from sin. The relationship with people, society, nation and state, is shaped by respect for parents and elders, the drive for justice and truth, honouring one's teachers, and obedience to the State *(sic)*. People take good care of the natural environment and exploit it for their common welfare. The social-cultural environment that fosters the worship of God must be safeguarded. This worship includes respect for teachers and the obligation to honour and be devoted to parents; this is expressed in manners and behaviour.

In other words, this first lesson about obedience emphasizes the student's subjection to what is more exalted than him or herself. Such subordination implies obedience as a religious act that is given shape by submission to God, state, nation, society, teachers, and parents. Implicitly, these are presented as a totality worthy of worship: it is this devotion that brings about its harmony. This makes, therefore, the individual behaviour of the student important. It must be reined in through obsequious submission.

The chapter called 'Concern' is about rights and duties. It opens with the observation that religious persons will be able clearly to discern rights from obligations. Controlled by religious teachings, they may be expected to strike the right balance in exercising their rights and duties. 'In a general way, people's rights and obligations in the world are the same. For instance, everybody has the right to be protected by the state. He is also obliged to create harmony in life'. Regarding national life and the state, such rights and obligations have been laid down in the Constitution and other regulations; they should be practised in harmonious unity, that is, in the spirit of Pancasila.

Referring to the Constitution of 1945, people are said to be equal before the law and the government, and must hold up said law and government. In other words, offenders will be prosecuted by the state; people are not allowed to take the law into their own hands. All people have the right to work, and to receive a reasonable wage, in proportion to their skills and education. People enjoy the freedoms of association and expression within the bounds of the law. This demonstrates that our state guarantees democratic life. This means that all Indonesians have the right to associate in organizations that strive to develop and educate the nation. Opinions must be advanced through the right channels, such as Parliament. This is in conformity with the principles of mutual consultation in order to reach unanimity *(azas musyawarah mufakat)*, and of national stability.

While the above concerns political rights and obligations, we also find them in the field of the economy. The Constitution stipulates that economic life is a joint effort, based on the family principle, in which the state must control those branches of production that directly affect the livelihood of the people, alongside the country's natural resources, in order to promote the people's welfare. This means that cooperatives suit us best. There, the application of the family principle results in the fact that enterprises are run by and for the members, and thus for the common interest. (It is not explained how these ideas about economic organization affect rights and obligations.) In the social-cultural field people have the right to education, which the government must provide. This is important to develop human resources. It is crucial to develop national culture too. Our national culture is composed of the best things the regional cultures have to offer; they constitute the root of our personality. Therefore, we have the duty to ward off negative outside influences that destroy Indonesian culture.

Finally, there are rights and duties concerning national defence, and the maintenance of peace and stability. National stability — so important for development, and to guarantee our rights and duties — is not just the Army's responsibility. In our neighbourhood organization (*RT*), we have watch duty; at school we must see to a peaceful study environment. From all this follows that we shall strive to shape persons who are Pancasilaists, and who are deeply concerned about all problems that occur in our land.

> To shape the Pancasila man is an expression of concern about consciousness of being a nation and a state. This attitude is based on the understanding that it is important to maintain a balance between rights and duties, and must be instilled from an early age. Why is this so? Because God urges people to do good and be pious. All good deeds receive God's reward. Human life is not for oneself alone. People must sympathize with the suffering of others, because they do not live alone on this planet. At the same time this attitude expresses how important it is to let duty prevail over right.

We must be conscious of, and appreciate the extreme diversity of, the Indonesian population. Yet, in spite of this, throughout the islands we find the spirit of mutual help, of gotong-royong. In order to shape our Unity in Diversity, we must endeavour to understand the regional cultures in the spirit of gratefulness to God to have endowed us with such a rich land. This should goad us to shape our destiny through Development. Regarding this national endeavour, we all have the same rights and obligations, irrespective of ethnicity, religion, descent, and origin. Our national development is inspired by, and the fulfilment of, the Trilogy of Development that stipulates equitable distribution of the benefits of growth, the necessity of economic progress, alongside dynamic and sound national stability. These three principles form an inseparable unity; it is the lodestar of our national economic effort.

Under 'Adherence to the Rules', a cardinal principle is reiterated. People are social creatures. While all of us have our peculiarities, we must live together and need each other; we must cooperate. People going their own way may disturb the harmony and good neighbourship of life. In order to avoid this, we need common norms to hold to. Such norms consist of rules and regulations that bring about order and acceptable behaviour. All members of society must conform to the prevailing norms. As good members of the state, in possession of Pancasila morality, we know we have to conform to and obey the legitimate regulations. Then both personal and communal desires can easily be fulfilled. After all, the law develops with and reflects the social will.

Development, in all its aspects, materially and spiritually, is the necessary condition to reach a just and prosperous society. It requires the participation of all. It also demands the spirit of change in order to attain a modern society. This entails influences from the outside world. Thanks to Pancasila, we can separate the good from the less desirable. Development must conform with the direction, goal, and ideals of our national struggle, such as proclaimed in the Preamble of the Constitution of 1945. There it has — among other things — been declared that we intend to reach prosperity and social justice. This is not the responsibility of the Government alone; all must feel accountable and play their part, by caring for the weak, and by utilizing science and technology. In this sense, development begins with personal, familial, and communal development: people themselves are its very subject. This must be paired with the attitudes of service, obedience, and discipline regarding the interests of state and nation.

According to the said Preamble, the Indonesian nation has been established to realize certain objectives, such as prosperity, astuteness, and an orderly world based on freedom, eternal peace, and social justice. This unity of purpose makes each Indonesian feel part of the whole, which results in the spirit of familism. This spirit animates all aspects of life, and is reflected in mutual help, appreciation, respect, and cooperation. All this will create harmony among us, despite religious diversity, but also because religion teaches us to restrain ourselves. It is, therefore, important to promote religious life, tolerance, and national unity. Concord should be our highest aim; we should sympathize with each other; we should do as we would be done by.

God does not discriminate between people. In the same spirit, the Pancasila acknowledges people's equality in terms of rank, rights, and obligations. Consciousness of this equality results in self-respect and awareness of basic rights. Such basic human rights comprise the rights to life, freedom, and property. These rights reflect the stage of cultural progress reached. Nowadays, basic rights concern (1) private rights, among others, the freedom of religion, of worship, of association and expression; (2) economic rights, such as the freedoms to own, to buy and sell, and to choose an occupation; (3) the right to equality before the law and government; (4) political rights, such as equality and a voice in decision making, to found political parties, and to propose petitions, criticism, and advice; (5) the rights to education and cultural development; (6) protection against unlawful arrest and searches. These rights belong to people by nature; they are God's gift. As a result, and in gratefulness to God, these rights are inscribed in our Constitution.

We take pride in the fact that basic rights were spelled out in our original constitution, which was enacted on 18 August 1945, well ahead of the Universal Declaration of Human Rights of 10 December 1948. What is special about our basic rights is that we know them to be ordained by God in the recognition of the dignity, value, and rank of the human being as the most perfect creature in existence. Such rights are invested in people. The right to sovereignty — and freedom from foreign interference — is vested in the state. This sovereignty belongs to the people, and is given shape by its representatives. This people's sovereignty — meaning that the people are the source of state power — leads to democracy, which is an old Indonesian custom anyway. Our democracy is guided by the values of the Pancasila that constitutes our ideology and national world view. As a result, we respect the Constitution and the rule of law, and reject absolute government. Pancasila democracy is further characterized by mutual consultation to reach unanimous agreement that is animated by the spirit of familism and mutual assistance. As a result, decisions will not be in conflict with personal interests.

Our Parliament decides on the basis of musyawarah, and its decisions are thus binding on all people in Indonesia. They must obey, respect, and execute the law faithfully. This is true not only for the regulations of the state: in family and village we also reach agreement by way of consultation. All this demonstrates that people are actively involved — and must involve themselves — in the affairs of state and national development. The last endeavour is nothing else but a fulfilment of the promise of Pancasila, and results in the creation of the Complete Indonesian Man. The Pancasila is our point of departure, and our guide.

Pancasila teaches us that happiness flows from concord, harmony, and balance in human relationships, and thus we need to exercise self-control as members of groups. We should give shape to our positions in life through awareness. This means that we should be conscious of others and put the interests of nation and state before our own. Since we are all equal, it won't do to force one's will on others. On the contrary, we must respect each other, and be guided by truth and justice. In that way, we will be able to execute our duties to our own benefit. It will lead us to be highly conscious of our group life, in the awareness that our private will is confined by the common interest. If, however, people start pushing forward their own interests at the expense of others, harmony, and the feeling of togetherness, will be lost.

To maintain social awareness and responsibility, we need norms. Knowing and respecting these is to say that we are cultured and civilized, which equates with the ideals that are the foundation of the Pancasila and Constitution of 1945. To live up to norms and regulations results in peaceful and quiet conditions. This begins in the family, and then spreads to wider circles of association. This shaping of culture goes together with an ever-increasing self-awareness, and thus with a growing sense of service to community and society. It is, therefore, in the adaptation to the social environment that people can experience and realize their human value and basic rights; true self-realization results in harmonious unity between self and environment. From such respect for order, happiness flows; it results in a dynamic yet peaceful society in which all of us take an active part.

If a nation is to be conscious of its unity and continuity, it needs a world view that suggests direction and solutions. Our world view is the Pancasila; it is the condensation of our national personality. On several occasions, the strength of Pancasila has been tested by rebellions and separatist movements. Their failure proves that the Indonesian people desire Pancasila as the foundation of the nation, that it has the power to unite all of us. As the basis of the nation, Pancasila is the source of our law. It gives purpose and direction. It animates our national soul. Its five principles are forged into one unit, complete in itself, which cannot be broken up into pieces. It is the noble promise of our people, contained in the depth of our hearts. As a result, it spurs on our desire for national unity and our sense of belonging together. This has been formulated in the *Wawasan Nusantara* — the archipelago concept — that affirms that we form a oneness of ideology, politics, economy, society and culture, and of defence and peace keeping, in short *Ipoleksosbudhankam*, which is tied to the integrity of our territory, that is of our land, sea, and airspace. To maintain these, on the basis of Pancasila, is the realization of our nation.

At school, Pancasila education aims at the construction of the complete Indonesian man, who is full of belief in and devotion to God, tolerant of others, and who subordinates self-interest to the common welfare. This is the purpose of our national development effort, too. We want to see mature people in a progressing society. Development is, therefore, not merely concerned with material things, such as food and housing, but also with inner happiness, education, peace and justice. In other words, development is a total package in which all play their parts, and which unites the nation while directing it to its destination. Still, we need vigilance and tolerance because, sometimes, the spirit of ethnicity, of chauvinism, extremism and provincialism, emerges, and threatens our integrity and nationalism. This regularly occurred under the old dispensation. Nowadays, however, we have achieved a high level of togetherness, in which the interests of nation and state take precedence over religious, group, and regional interests. We have been successful in resurrecting our national personality.

Together we constitute one big family. This is reflected in our practice of mutual consultation, mutual help, and economic cooperation. We live by the family principle. As in the family, we have mutually unequal tasks and duties, the execution of which serves the common welfare. The good child must, therefore, always honour parents and elders, refrain from saying whatever it likes, and restrain itself from irritating others. Politeness is mandatory in everyday life.

Being subjected to group decisions is softened by the reassurance that personal authoritarianism has no place in Pancasila society.

Besides, considerations of equality regularly surface too. Sometimes reference is made to universal human rights; we also encounter sentences such as 'Freedom is something that relates to the human essence, and entails physical and spiritual aspects, alongside the elements of dignity and human values', and 'In our social, national, and state life, all nationals have the right to equality of dignity and prestige'. As a result, the Indonesian nation is said to not discriminate between its citizens. All of them have the same rank, rights and obligations in a harmonious society. This is the meaning of the second Pancasila principle, 'just and civilized humanity'. It boils down to the recognition of human dignity; of justice; of the qualities of creativity, feeling, will, and conviction. Therefore, the interindividual differences we observe in everyday life only show that there are differences in tasks and duties. This is underlined in our laws. We are a constitutional country, respecting freedoms and basic rights. These may be enjoyed in a responsible manner, without taking advantage of others, without arbitrariness, and without causing conflicts and cleavages that endanger our unity and integrity. On the other hand, the principle of equality — together with our love for the nation — is a powerful appeal to eradicate poverty, misery and discrimination from our midst.

> Necessity/God's will ordains that people, as social beings, must be ready to sacrifice. Total *(lahir dan batin)* happiness can only be attained when we experience harmony, smoothness, and equilibrium. To attain these, we need to be ready to sacrifice. This readiness serves the interests of humanity, and of our society, nation and state.

In our Revolution, patriots went a long way in bringing sacrifices; many of them even offered their lives. These days, we have to pay contributions and taxes, and to help each other in making social progress. We must also accept decisions taken in the name of the common good and for the sake of development. Accepting these decisions demonstrates our feelings of social solidarity. These feelings were readily brought to the fore by the willingness of the population of Kedung Ombo when they sacrificed their land for the sake of a reservoir, that is to say, for the sake of nation and state.

The New Order arose in response to the unrest of the early years of independence. In those days, our unity was threatened by all sorts of conflicts; by unlimited freedom; liberal, West-imitating policies; aliran politics. All of this led to the political stalemate that finally resulted in Guided Democracy. Then basic freedoms were suppressed; the country spiralled down into inexorable chaos. The new regime understood the need for a firm ideological direction: when people were animated by the spirit of Pancasila democracy, problems would dissolve and development proceed. This meant basic political retooling; people's participation; democratic consciousness; Pancasila training; the strengthening of Parliament; clean and authoritative government. The first conditions to be fulfilled were to establish national stability; to organize elections; to choose President and Vice-President; and to create a free and responsible press.

Even though we have been quite successful on so many fronts, we still need to be on guard to defend our independence and attainments. The fight against colonialism resulted in an environment where humanitarianism and justice could flourish. To maintain these, and to realize our national progress, we need to practise the Pancasila and Constitution of 1945, and to be vigilant. We need vigilance in five areas. In the field of ideology, it is important to have a strong world view, based on the Pancasila that has already proven its potency and sacred qualities. In the political field, we should be guided by popular will and Pancasila ideology. In the economy, we must be on guard against liberalism and the profit motive. After all, the cooperative principle is the central pillar of our economic life. In the social-cultural field, we must cultivate loyalty and solidarity, and be wary of conspicuous consumption, the gap between rich and poor, and jealousy among groups: the latter can easily cause a social tempest. Concerning defence and peace keeping, it is clear that all of us have our roles to play. We should be alert to everything that might disturb our peace and order.

Besides watchfulness, the Pancasila teaches us to foster the spirit of the family and mutual help; to be just; to balance rights with obligations; to be respectful of others; to be generous; to avoid exploiting others; not to be wasteful; not to live in extravagance; to respect the public interest; to like hard work; not to be jealous; to participate in creating a progressive and socially just environment.

The Development-oriented complete Indonesian human beings, the real Pancasila men, are nation builders. They are people animated by the spirit of Pancasila, they have been touched by it. They are inspired by the unity and integrity of Indonesia, and are willing to sacrifice for it. They are honest and sincere, not striving after their self-interest, but equating it with the interest of all. Their sense of duty makes them exemplary leaders who inspire other people. Their identification with the group is like the ideal unity of government and people. It results in the stable and dynamic oneness of economy, politics, the social-cultural field, defence and peace keeping. If our youth, as the successor generation of our lofty ideals, shall carry on the good work, they can be said to be Pancasila-inspired nation builders. To create these is the very purpose of Pancasila education.

Naturally, such nation builders have a high sense of discipline. Ultimately, it is from the self-discipline of each and everybody that national discipline, and thus national unity, follow. In the first place, such discipline seems to entail obedience, or obsequiousness, to the normative order of social life. At a deeper level, it means the training of the batin, or one's character, in order to be in step with the order. This will result in development. Discipline mirrors civilization: the more mature a nation, the higher its respect for the rules. A developed society is a well-regulated society. Thus, whereas by nature individuals strive to fulfil their self-interest, in society they become conscious of the benefit of harmony and conformity, without yet losing their essential being. After all, mastery of the self leads to the realization of the common welfare, and to the harmonious unity of social life from which individual happiness flows. As a result, as private persons, all nationals also fulfil their basic obligations, such as strengthening their religious life; serving nation and state; being devoted to parents, teachers, and humanity. These noble duties are most proper to cultivate.

In the main, these are the messages harped on about during the last four years at school. Yet, it may still be useful to consider the material, and its reasoning, for the final grade. In doing this, we should bear in mind that the material offered is directed at seventeen and eighteen-year olds who have been flooded with Pancasila thinking throughout their school experience. It seems, therefore, reasonable to hope that loose ends are finally tied together, and that an adult student can make some sense of it all.

Under 'Concord' we are informed — probably for the six-hundredth time, estimating that it occurs at least once a week, and over twelve years — that people need each other, and thus had better live in peace and cooperate with and accept each other. 'Religion can unite and synchronize all human activities, both individually, and as a member of the group'. 'In establishing social life, the Indonesian Man will always ... obey, submit to, and honour elders ... and refrain from free sex because it is against the religious teachings and against national culture, and also because it may cause infection by AIDS'. 'Concord is the mental attitude in the scheme of shaping harmonious life that does not differentiate between rank, socio-economic position, and differences in religion and belief in God'.

Extremism is the strongest form of egoism, such as demonstrated by the communists. 'The PKI clearly wanted to force its will upon others by justifying all means of reaching its political objectives'; 'Basically, people want to do as they please. However, in practice, they are bound by their limitations and responsibility for the environment, society and state. For instance, this is illustrated by the desires to associate with one another, to obtain an education, to be equal before the law, and suchlike'. Apart from fighting egoism, the New Order also has a few things to promote:

> Another endeavour of the New Order is to heighten the meaning and sense of the Archipelago Concept. Wawasan Nusantara is the concept in our thinking about national development that includes the natural realm — which consists of the geographical position, the natural abundance, the number of people — and also the social aspects, which cover the political-ideological, the social and cultural, and the economic, along with the defence and security aspects [of the country as a whole]. Wawasan means 'view, consideration, or way of looking or considering'. Nusantara is the terrirory of the Indonesian state that consists of three unitary elements, namely the far-flung archipelago; the territorial waters; and the airspace that spreads out above the groups of islands and our waters, which comprises land, sea and air as a complete unity. In this way, Wawasan Nusantara is the way the Indonesian nation looks at itself and its surround-

ings that is based on the Pancasila and Constitution of 1945 in order to give shape to the purpose of national development ... One political unit also means that the Pancasila is the only philosophy and ideology of the state ... Socio-cultural oneness also means that Indonesian culture is essentially one.

In the modern world, cultural contact is inevitable, and often invigorating. As long as foreign cultural elements are grafted on the national identity that is firmly rooted in the practice of Pancasila, no problems will occur. Yet, next to this concern of being led astray by foreign culture, we find four other contemporary problems that need to be tended to: (1) the imbalance between *pribumi* (ethnic) and non-ethnic Indonesians, and (2) the imbalance between foreign and local capital. The first problem should not arise; after all, we want to be united, 'because basically the Government offered the freedom to all its subjects to do their utmost to realize the common welfare'. The second problem is that our people are relatively backward in comparison with the developed countries. To solve this condition, we must study and learn from the experiences of other nations. (3) The third problem has been stated earlier, namely, the fact that the country is being flooded by foreign ideas. The Pancasila should function as a filter to separate the good from the bad. (4) The last point does not concern any problem at all, yet follows the 'logic' of the book. It is the recommendation 'to work for the continuity of the noble cultural values of the Indonesian nation which demands that we must steadily increase their practice'.

The last recommendation can be realized by developing and caring for the regional cultures: it is these that are deeply rooted and really alive. They contain religious, humanitarian, unifying, and collectivistic elements that should be strengthened. The unity of the nation can be promoted by exchanging cultural and artistic missions. In that way, groups who were formerly isolated can receive new cultural elements. 'Another manner that can support the quest for elements from and the development of regional culture is to collect its art in the expectation that regional culture is a part of the national one'. The examples given concern dances, songs and tunes.

The next chapter is about 'Loyalty' or 'Obedience'. It explains Pancasila democracy. Indonesia is democratic; this we can see from the

Constitution in which it is written that sovereignty is in the hands of the people; it is exercised by Parliament. The part the people play is thus most important. They take their decisions through that very Indonesian mechanism of musyawarah: common action is based on common decisions. 'The identity of Pancasila democracy is its fourth principle that is inspired by the first, second, third and fifth principles of the Pancasila. Conceptually, therefore, Pancasila democracy reflects the values of the Pancasila'.

Connected with these values is the idea that everybody enjoys the freedom of association and expression. We solve problems by talking about them; we negotiate until we reach unanimous agreement. Opinion that expresses the will and interest of the people must come out on top. This we Indonesians have been doing since time immemorial. Of course, reaching agreement must be done in ways that avoid conflict and confrontation. Our press is responsible, and as a people we have reached maturity. We thus negotiate in the spirit of familism and cooperation. This means that we depart from the premiss that the national interest always takes precedence over individual or group interests. Finally, to reach dynamic stability, we need a well-regulated society, and everybody must submit to, obey, and be obsequious to the regulations concerned. It is through obeying the prevailing regulations that we express our respect for our fellows. In the end this will lead to a just and prosperous society based on the Pancasila.

The chapters about religious tolerance and conviction stress that life in Indonesia is based on belief in God, from which it seems to follow that Indonesian nationals are expected to embrace one religion or another [five are officially recognized]. In this choice, these nationals are free. The freedom to embrace a religion is the most basic of the basic human rights. Yet, one is not free not to embrace a religion. After all, belief in God is the moral basis of the state, and so it must also be that of its individual subjects. In the theory of the state, it is seen as, 'People who have a strong religious conviction will have a positive influence on secure and stable national life, because we are convinced that people who really believe and are devout will certainly love their fatherland and state'. This obviously needs to be given further shape in the practice of the Pancasila, which seems to have grown to become the sacred ally of religion, or rather, religion appears as the sanctifier of

Pancasila. Once again this is stressed in the idea that belief in God animates the other principles; they would be lifeless without that soul. [If one wonders how this is intrinsic to the ideas of humanitarianism, democracy, social justice, and national unity, then that merely reveals that one still has a long way to go in becoming the Complete Indonesian Man.] The Pancasila man knows that divinity is not an invention of people's minds and intentions, but that the concept of divinity is known to men through revelation.

In a dissertation about familism, it is asserted that Indonesians do not behave according to the *homo homini lupus* principle, but as *homo homini socius*. This seems to mean that a community is a unit that cannot be split into smaller units, and that individuals, as equals, are fully integrated into it. The eternal village serves to illustrate this, yet, also in town, people still stick to familism and cooperation. These are also the principles of the national economy. In the question section, social relationships in modern society suddenly appear to be based on material compensation. The student is asked to give his opinion about this, as well as about the statement: 'In urban society where people are very busy, the spirit of familism is not always necessary'.

In spite of all the blessings the eternal Pancasila bestows on the Indonesian nation, there appear to be some problems too. The spirit of materialism stands in the way of intimate relationships. After all, its main motivation is money. It further leads to status competition, and thus discrimination. Money makes a person special. The spirit of secularism is problematic, too. It reflects worldliness. It leads to the separation of worldly and ultimate concerns; to the separation of state and religion. Undesirable individualism is a consequence of the progress of technology and communication. People serve their own interests only, and thus compete, which leads to the situation where the poor lose out. The fourth undesirable condition is elitism, which means the existence of groups who feel themselves to be much superior to ordinary people because of power, position, and wealth. Wouldn't it therefore be better if the nation closed itself off? Well, as a state striving for progress, this is not possible; even if it was wanted, globalization would prevent it. We have to follow with the times. Besides, our progress is impressive because we stick to Pancasila, and 'The smoothness, harmony and equilibrium of human life and Indonesian society, in their fullest sense, are ever developing'. We are progressing on all fronts, and as long as national security and stability are maintained, we have nothing to fear. Still, we should restrain the spirit of feudalism, of exclusivism, and narrow-minded regionalism. Next to these, let us be suspicious of foreign values that are in opposition to our culture.

However much things appear to be in order to reach the twenty-first century and the Complete Indonesian Man, there remain some obstacles. One would be the tendency to close the country off from the rest of the world, such as under Guided Democracy, which clearly resulted in an atmosphere of authoritarianism and totalitarianism. This is a non-issue, though: 'We do not find this during New Order times and so there is no reason for us not to be prepared to welcome the era of the Second National Awakening'. Another obstacle to national development is the culture of depending on the government. Similarly obstructive are the nonprogressive attitudes of pessimism, fatalism, and nonparticipation in social affairs. What is most needed now is the participation of all: the people should be made the subject of development, and not merely its object. Apart from the government-dependent attitude, there are other ones that stand in the way of the development of the pioneering, independent person that the future Indonesian Man has been intended to be. Many still take 'short-cuts' in promoting their self-interest, bribing their way while disregarding the law. Others operate under the protection of powerful patrons, and do very much as they please. Then there are those who take their social responsibilities lightly; they do not care about others and only see their own material interests. Yet, loyalty and submission to Pancasila, the Constitution of 1945, state and Government shall overcome these negative attitudes. With a firm basis in Pancasila, 'the Indonesian people will become *monodualistik* in the double sense of being individuals and mutually equal social beings in line with the Indonesian identity'.

The last chapter summarizes the oft-repeated statements about what the Pancasila state means, and it may still be useful to reproduce the main clauses. Pancasila democracy (1) is neither individualistic nor liberal, neither based on the people as a group, nor is it a class democracy; (2) it is not a mass democracy that looks at the people as social beings only; (3) it is 'monodualistic', the gist of which lies in familism. (4) It is constitutional, too. The familism principle can still be seen in the villages where the government functionaries feel to be one with the people, always caring for social unity and equilibrium. As a principle of state, this finds its expression in the idea of the *integralistik*, unitary state that transcends the various group-based views. The theory of the integralistic state does not place the state in isolation from its members as individuals, nor from their associations and groups. Yet, all groups and individuals must be conscious that together they form one system in the order of government, while the state must uphold the unity that binds them all.

Thus the New Order gives shape to Pancasila democracy, the essence of which lies (1) in familism, the Indonesian nation being one big family; (2) in the rejection of individualism; (3) in the discarding of the theory of class struggle. (4) It is based on the theory of the integralistic state; (5) in which the people, as democratic subjects, have the right to voice their opinion; (6) through elections and parliament. This manner of free expression demonstrates self-restraint and a great measure of social responsibility. (7) Pancasila leadership moves us on to our destiny, and is legitimized by the consistent application of Pancasila democracy; (8) this is also expressed in the government's relationships with social and political organizations. (9) We reach our decisions through musyawarah negotiations, not through the application of might; (10) such decisions reflect the totality and unanimity of opinion; (11) in this way we avoid majority and minority groups, and the problems of opposition and conflicting interests do not occur.

Mysticism? Mystification?

To reiterate: it is not my purpose to comment here on the substance of the Pancasila and civics course. In the preceding section, I tried to offer the reader the core ideas as they are presented at school. Even when attempting to present the gist, distilled from four year-course books, it was difficult to avoid repetition. In view of the fact that the students are exposed to basically the same material for twelve years in a row, the reader may begin to wonder what this time and effort is all about. Well, to belabour without end seems to serve indoctrination. The same method is at the basis of the teaching of ethics: the same recommendations and prescriptions recur time and again, until they are supposed to have sunk in. Then the father has handed his knowledge over to his sons, and so on. Besides, as a method, this practice is very much part of the idea of education: values, as *dharmashastra*, need to be taught to be memorized; learning is rote learning.

As such — call it indoctrination, or the teaching of ethics — the method of presentation is nothing new. And this brings us precisely to the point of our present exercise. Is there much that is new in Pancasila and civics education? Is it merely a rehash of older ideas? According to my impression, it is almost like listening to certain mystical masters, such as I did in the past. Things appear to have been made mystical, nebulous, secretive. What is clear and simple does not seem to be interesting. By cloaking it in mystery — for instance, by reducing everything to One — things become more true, as it were, and then stand in need of being revealed. Is this mysticism? Or is it mystification? What I am struck by is the correspondence between Javanese kebatinan thinking and the way Pancasila morality is argued. I do not say that one is the same as the other, or that there is a causal relationship. Yet both seem to hail from the same cultural kitchen somewhere in South-Central Java. The cooking has a related taste; the way the food has been flavoured reveals its origin. To many Indonesians, this may constitute just another instance of Javanization.

Let us trace the parallels. It is fun. And let us give the pride of place to the teacher. We have noted that the Pancasila course repeatedly emphasizes that parents, teachers, and the state need to be respected. This is a cardinal moral imperative — in priyayi mystical parlance, it is a way of honouring 'God', to whom, after all, all destinies aspire. Teachers are part of the moral hierarchy; it is through them, or rather, their wisdom, that people may be guided on the path, whether through life or supernature. In this case the teacher — say, the headmaster — is the state, the embodiment of the raja, the king. It is hoped that such rulers have a wahyu, that they share in revelation, in truth, and thus speak words of wisdom. Similarly, in the same way as Mangkunegara IV wrote his acclaimed Wédhatama to instruct his sons; and as President Soeharto shared his insights with his children — and the public — when he published *Butir-butir Budaya Jawa* (*Grains of Javanese Wisdom*, 1990), the state teaches its wards the ethics of life. It teaches Pancasila philosophy.

In relation to their teachers, pupils are people who have not yet been formed. They are still ignorant, and need to be given the provisions they need on their journey through life: they need civilization, to be polished. Thus, in the same way as young Javanese children, or strangers, or drunkards for that matter, are considered to be durung jawa, not yet Javanese, so are nonindoctrinated children to be considered as durung, or rather, *belum Indonesia*, not yet Indonesian. They still need to be disabused and enlightened. To them, it is good to know that Indonesia has been revealed, and that it is stored in sacred formulations, of which the Pancasila and Constitution of 1945 are the deepest and most important. And since Indonesia is the shared possession of all, its owners have the right — and the duty — to be enlightened and to become real Indonesians, whole Pancasila men.

Wholeness, completeness, oneness — unity and integrity — is a very pervasive theme. The state equates with the government, which equates with the regime; the state equates with the nation, which equates with society. They are one, and one family, in which the inspired father teaches his wisdom. He scrutinizes the revealed mantras, explains them, then listens to the chorus that repeats them. Indonesia equates with government and state, with policies and population, with economy and geography, with culture and defence, with territory and people. It is all One. This oneness is in its Independence, in Pancasila, in Supersemar, and in the inseparable Trilogy of Development; it is in monodualitas and monoloyalitas. Whereas these formulae may, in some, elicit reminiscences of the corporate state, it is explained that the oneness of Indonesia is different: it is its overcoming of diversity, its realizing its inner dimensions, and reaching the goal of wholeness.

This wholeness has been explained in a variety of ways. It is organic wholeness, meaning that each and everybody has his or her function and place. People depend on each other; cannot be considered in separation from each other; they naturally belong together. Wholeness is integralistic, it integrates into a totality which is more than the constituent parts. This totality is the state. Wholeness is in familism, in the belonging to a graded group that inspires the desire to be together; it evokes the warmth of togetherness; wholeness becomes wholesomeness, too.

The individual is considered to be an integral part of the group, almost impossible to conceive of in independence. The individual person fuses with the group, and his moral task in life is to realize this fusion. The fact that persons are individually different, that they have wills, special qualities, opinions, and suchlike, is acknowledged. They may even have specific, position-bound prerogatives and obligations. The point is to exercise all these for the good of the encompassing totality: such is self-realization. In this thinking, the totality encompasses the individual, who realizes himself by encompassing the totality.

This is similar to the fusion between servant and Lord, mystic and 'God', and, in terms of government, between empathizing leader and the people under his care. This simile is nothing new. The loyal priyayi servant seeks to be one with his king, submits fully to the order of state and royal command, faithfully executing his task. This leads to the highest rewards; overcoming the self — its drives, emotions, rationality — frees it to fuse and to enjoy harmony in conformity with what is greater. This experience of harmony, of fusion, fills him up to equating with the totality; he becomes it, encompasses it. Container and contained are one. Government is the people, the people are the government. Servant and Lord, kawula and gusti, have absorbed each other.

Seen from the point of view of the lord, say, the state, the idealization of this priyayi ethic of the past is not just mystical; it is practical, too. It allows for the teaching of individual subordination to family, community, society, nation and state, which somehow, like Russian dolls, seem to fit into each other as microcosm fits into macrocosm. The mystically perfect man, the *insan kamil*, is in step with both all and one — his laku has been perfected. In a similar vein, Pancasila education offers the pupil endless series of rules on how to behave, how to practise, that is, on how to bring his laku in line with the encompassing society/state. In doing so, it apparently zeroes in on the elemental and the highest levels of practice. The lowest, shari'a, stresses the execution of rules, obedience to commands, and the routine of ritual; it means acceptance as the first step to deeper experience. Basically, it is discipline and disciplining the self. Then it jumps to the highest stage, the experience of tranquil harmony as the condition of happiness and self-realization: it is reaching the stage of the Complete Indonesian Man, and Pancasila society.

The good thing is that the latter two have already been revealed. They are contained in 'Pancasila' and 'Constitution of 1945'. These spell origin-and-destination. As mantras, they spellbind. As mantras, they cannot be changed, and will evoke what they have been destined to evoke. They are origin and destination at the same time, making the whole development effort appear as a mere pause on the road, an insignificant moment 'to take a drink', to refresh oneself.

The teaching of ethics as values and rules fits with the image of mantras. First of all, such values are thought to be preconditions for order. They must be made to work to achieve it. They do so by being inserted into individuals, who will feel that such values and rules attune them to the whole. In a way, it makes them wise — the wise man not being so stupid as to disturb social equilibrium. Why? Well, of course, it would disturb his own, and that would be stupid; wise people do not commit stupid actions. It is, therefore, deep down, that individual development counts: the batin, the 'character' needs to be trained, to be sensitized to the whole, from which the wilingness follows to serve society, nation and state — to serve the whole, up to humanity. Such is true self-realization. It is the full actualization of 'sepi ing pamrih, ramé ing gawé; mamayu hayuning buwana'.

In other words, under the right conditions, values are like mantras. They bring about what they are intended for. Origin will result in destination; destination results in origin. This receives an even heavier stress in the emphasis on regulations. The cosmos is a regulated, ordered whole; it is well coordinated, excluding chance; things happen as preordained co-incidental occurrences. Thus, knowing and declaring the right rules must bring order in their wake. This is even demonstrated in civilization, 'being cultured already', as opposed to the immature child who does not know the rules 'yet'. The right rules 'enspell' order, and make respect for its representatives — parents, guru, raja, State — spontaneous. Respect becomes laku *pur sang*.

The possibility of this Javanist interpretation of the substance of the Pancasila course is indeed fascinating and, in itself, reminiscent of Javanist practice. We do not need to bend over backwards to note the recurrent themes of harmony = adaptation = conformity with powerful formulae. The idea that values and rules bring about their own result is inspired more by magic than functionalism. Such values and rules —

Pancasila and Constitution — have been revealed, and are to bring about their own achievement. Thus, people had better adapt themselves to what is indeed inevitable. Indonesians must thus live according to the *kepribadian nasional*, the national personality, resulting in the complete Indonesian. Perfection has been preordained — thus it can, and will, be reached.

The state of perfection seems to be the state of total oneness — the accomplishment of the encompassing and complete truth of O, of kasunyatan, in which everything is still and clear, one and integrated. It is like the mufakat of the musyawarah, the totality and fulness, 'roundness', of the unanimity among men. It is harmony to the fullest. To bring this about, some teaching is needed. It is the act of social engineering in which values are manipulated, and the way in which this is done reminds us of the world of thought of kebatinan mysticism. In that individual-centred world, persons are made important, they can realize themselves, and, in spite of themselves, bring about social harmony. In Pancasila education, this sequence seems to have been reversed, and the self-realizing individual has somehow disappeared in the — harmonious — totality of the state. Thus, while the exercise of kebatinan is the striving for self-realization per se — irrespective of social demands — this promise does not mature in the ideas of the organic-integralistic state.

CHAPTER 8

Pancasila philosophy and society

The Pancasila was a great invention. Along with the mandatory flag, anthem, constitution, Declaration of Independence, and stories of resistance, it has evolved into the prime emblem of the nation. To many or most Indonesians, Pancasila is destiny, incorporating national identity and its related philosophy of life. As such, the invention of the Pancasila was felicitous; it became an effective tool for nation building and, sometimes, the envy of certain fellow Southeast Asians conscious of not being in possession of such a powerful myth of nationhood.

Until the time the State imposed its *final* interpretation of the Pancasila, Pancasilalogy was good fun. In any single year, many treatises appeared; certain professors became nationally famous exegists; others expounded on the parallels between local proverbs and the putative qualities of the five principles; others still recognized it as a revelation, and went into esoteric deciphering; certain mystical groups were founded in its name; 'laboratories' appeared to experiment with Pancasila; there was even talk about establishing a Faculty of Pancasilalogy. Many of these activities were given to magnify the mysterious dimensions of the five *sila*, Ketuhanan in itself readily offering a vast field of speculation. The five-is-really-one idea could prosper too, and definitely agreed with ideas about the organic-integralistic state, and the integrity and solidarity contained in the family principle.

In a way, the current official interpretation has maintained, yet frozen, the esoteric explanations, at the same time as the formula has been drawn back to earth, not only becoming the unique ideological basis of all organizational life, but also the moral measuring rod for all sorts of activities. At least, Pancasila is thought to be so: the source from which all Indonesian law emanates. In itself, such thinking is quite mystical, and we have seen that this potential is readily recognizable in the teachings of the state doctrine. The correspondence between these teachings and the world of thought of kebatinan mysticism, evokes more important, and pertinently practical, questions, too.

In chapter five, we placed contemporary kebatinan thought in its social-historcal setting, and noted that — as we know it today — it is a product of late colonial court society. As the preoccupation of certain priyayi gentlemen, it made a good match with a static image of social organization. Within that social setting, individuals could achieve some mobility, moving from position to position, and thus enhance their status, but the structure in which they moved was a given. It was thought to constitute a well-ordered, and thus highly civilized, society. In order to conform to social demands, the practice of kebatinan proved to be wise. By training the inner self, people had little difficulty in living up to the ethics of place; it cultivated noble qualities, such as humility. In its deeper dimensions, it opened the doors to the experience of superior truth, liberating the self, as it were, from the clutches of a wooden society in which things were good when they were in place.

This society was morally constructed, which means a number of things. It entails a steady emphasis on obligation: the places people occupy impose duties. To fulfil these tasks is a noble endeavour. Obligations are to be fulfilled vis-à-vis certain other positions which, in this case, means to people you know personally. Being faithful in these duties creates harmony, and such conformity to harmony, or harmonious conformity, constituted a noble purpose in itself, *lair-batin* — outwardly so, and hopefully, in its inner dimensions. Conformity should be spontaneous, reflecting equanimity of inner being. Whereas this society centred in the ruler, its dynastic model basically reflects the ideal construct of the family, the most moral construct of them all. There, hierarchy comes naturally, and is thus moral in itself; filial piety becomes a logical imperative. Service to the father, the parents — and by extension, to the boss, to the patrimonial dynast — becomes self-fulfilment.

In other words, the social construct — the social imagination — results in a society that is harmonious, free of conflict, and part of the personal experience; it is anchored on execution of duty, and consciousness of place. The individual is defined by place and duties; subjected to the welfare — harmony — of the whole. In the current discussion, this is known as Asian Values.

We noted that the way Pancasila and civics are explained at school comes rather close to the moral model expounded above. The

Pancasila society which the government says it wants to realize, appears to be a collectivistic arrangement in which the individual is a subservient part of the whole. To make this attractive, people are promised the double reward of a harmonious totality, and personal fulfilment in conformity. People must thus be absorbed by society; it sounds almost like the mystical message of fusing self and 'God'. Be this as it may, the Pancasila teachings — much like kebatinan — seem to fit with a social construct that is well ordered, well regulated, and thus highly civilized. This was the priyayi ideal, it is true, of the past — yet it still has a familiar ring, in spite of the capital now being far from the Javanese heartland and the fact that there are no real priyayi left.

In other words, the civilizing mission that the Indonesian state engages in propagates messages that belong to an idealized past, with an idealized structure of society in which organic and integralistic ideas could flourish; subsequently, these ideas were formulated as the family principle. This principle animates one and all; it animates the collectivity. It results in a oneness of breath, in a 'rounded' totality. This image is said to reflect the national personality that is thought to be an essential part of each and everybody in the archipelago. In this essence, people are truly united. They share in its traits, they share in culture. And apparently, many people simply want to believe this. It agrees with how they think about their family, at least, how they feel about it. It seems as if their imagination does not reach beyond a highly personalistic society. Like the family, society must be a moral order and, if not yet so, it should become one.

To accomplish this, the state disseminates culture. It covers itself in culture, presents itself as such. It is the Great Teacher, displaying ceremony, election rituals, unanimous nominations, unity-in-diversity television shows, endless series of successful development projects, mantra-like speeches, uniforms and more uniforms, happy, family-planned families, cleanest villages, obsequious women called Ibu, grateful civil servants, and so on. Such manifestations are supposed to — and do — take the sights off political and economic decision making. They obscure social cleavages and concede considerable freedom to those few who indeed take the decisions.

In disseminating culture, the state sticks to the family principle in more than one way. In the family, it is true, small children are taught through repetition, through being told more than once what is expected of them, and how to behave. Besides, parents seem to have the means of drilling it in. The state follows up on this model, repeating the same values over and over again, apparently expecting them to stick, to sink in, and then to regulate behaviour 'spontaneously'. It calls itself a cultural order. It propagates basic change, which explicitly means change in values. Its social engineering is value engineering.

All great prophets, founders of religion, popes and preachers, have steadily made appeals to bring about a change of heart. If individuals repent, convert, and see their errors, they will experience redemption; they may even redeem the world. If all people are good, society must be in good order. This thinking is even older than the road to Rome. It has been with us since ancient times. The appeals are still made. It did not, and does not help much. Perhaps people are not given to wisdom; perhaps they are not driven by values. Perhaps the scheme, or the basic thinking behind it, is flawed.

Values, culture, thought, all of these are related to certain praxis; they do not lead a life of their own. As we have seen, kebatinan thinking, as we know it these days, had very much to do with developments in late colonial society — a society that was changing rapidly. It belonged to conservative court circles, and the lifestyle of the priyayi. It was, in part, a reaction to the flux of times, and a means of fitting in with the stifling environment of the palace. It grew to become an ideology, and served as a model for ideologizing. Now, children, pupils, students, civil servants, Ibu-ibu, all and sundry are bombarded with it. They are being filled with values that, possibly, make sense at school and in government offices but which, certainly, are out of step with praxis, with how life is lived on the other side of the school fence, or beyond official premises. Besides, everybody is aware of this discrepancy. There is a wide gap between state ideology and official knowledge, and everyday experience. Still, many people hope that, somehow, ideology and knowledge have the magic power to redress all society's ills. We have not achieved perfection yet — we expect to arrive at that final station, though. The ideal community is in reach. Complete Indonesian human beings can be constructed. Let us believe in being 'Javanese'. 'In our culture' we think this way; 'in our culture' we behave like this: we compromise, we are understanding, we give in, we are one big family.

This reasoning exposes the basic flaw. Indonesia is not a big family. In a family, you know each other personally. You do not know two-hundred-million people that way. Indonesia is not a community. It is, perhaps, a national economy, a so-called nation state, and it is conceptually difficult to call it a society. There are so many culturally specific groups, communities, and societies within Indonesia. And culture, or values, is no guide. It is the outcome of praxis, not its lodestar. If it has any worth, and if it can condition anything at all, then it must be close to praxis, to be relevant to it. Thus, if what is propagated in the name of culture and essential being clearly belongs to another era, it can never accomplish something relevant to present-day society. The best that can be hoped for, for the student, is a good grade; for the functionary, a promotion.

The ruralites know that current village society is no closely knit community any longer — if it ever was. In colonial times a normally steep stratification among villagers was common, and village decision making — in spite of deliberations — was far from democratic. The stir among the have-nots in the 1950s and 1960s made class antagonism blatantly visible. Economic development, the green revolution, and the incorporation of village leadership in the apparatus of the state, have exacerbated cleavages and, sometimes, strife. The eternal village of gotong-royong, musyawarah, and mufakat simply is not there.

Whereas villagers may still entertain face-to-face relationships — a way of defining community — urbanites have grown accustomed to operating in an anonymous society. They do not know each other any longer — and are not interested in doing so, either. In their environment, the pursuit of individual interests comes naturally. This is not so because they are morally defective people; on the contrary, they take good care of their families, and, given the chance, they may even be responsible citizens. The problem in Indonesian society is that government does not give this chance; it is very suspicious of people who think for themselves, of citizenship, of all forms of moral autonomy. The state wants to control its subjects, and tries to mould their minds.

Nobody is, of course, so naive as to deny social practice. We even noted that — occasionally — the Pancasila and civics course touches on certain problems. In earlier years, all of them were said to originate from communism, and from individual inclinations — in brief, from people who were not, or rather, who were still not, Pancasilaists. Over the last decade, communism, as the New Order's megaspook, has suffered from considerable deflation, although it still forms part of the vocabulary of certain military spokesmen. These days, 'individualism' and 'liberalism' are most often blamed for the social condition. Next to these, the threat from SARA issues, such as narrow-minded regionalism, religious intolerance, racial discrimination, and class antagonism, also makes it to the headlines, although normally in a subdued manner. After all, SARA problems have a very high explosive potential.

If we turn the course's teachings on their head by asking ourselves why certain things receive so much emphasis and reiteration, we can easily see that SARA, and unrestrained individuals, are persistently perceived as problems that must be placed under the spell of indoctrination. Yet, do not doubt that — behind the scenes — the state apparatus is very busy keeping the lid on tensions, and preferably, defusing them. We do not need to turn the course's substance on its head, though, to look for further acknowledgements that not everything develops in the direction of the Pancasila society. Quite a number of problems are squarely recognized as existing. All of them are undesirable. In the twelfth grade they were summarized; let us inspect them again.

It was lamented that urban living — and even the application of science and technology — gave rise to materialism, competition, discrimination, and individualism. I think that such observations can be made universally. Urban living sets one free from immediate social control and, thus, individualizes. The supply of all sorts of attractive products makes people want to own them. Their setting a price on gadgets and goods can be called materialism. Besides, most people work for (and pay for merchandise with) money. Money and material things become the measure. Since these do not come for free, people need to work hard, and to compete. Finally, their anonymous big-city environment makes them care for themselves and their immediate family members and associates. Who else is there to care for?

In this setting, it is not strange that some people succeed better than others. Some are smarter, some are closer to power and protection, and the poor stream in faster than jobs can be created. Many live in miserable conditions, while some at the higher end of the scale get rich and, sometimes, very rich. They normally mind their own affairs, like all the rest. As a result, we find a wide gap between rich and poor, between the haves and have-nots, and the chances of the latter are barely improving. This situation has, of course, everything to do with the type of development the country pursues, the privileges that — 'naturally' — accrue at the top, and the exploitative capitalist regime that prevails. Yet, such things go unmentioned — as also the structural commentary necessary to understand the basic observations about urban living. It is even suggested that the whole set of undesirable conditions is an import — presumably from the nefarious West — when it is proposed that such problems are so un-Indonesian, so un-Pancasilaist that the country can only protect itself from them by closing itself off from the globalizing world. Well, such is not within the bounds of practical possibility.

Whatever the causes, eminently Indonesian things appear to suffer and decline. Familism — that wonderful trait — seems to deteriorate because relationships are now measured in money. Even in families themselves, intimacy is diminishing, as people have less time for each other, and to spend together, than in earlier days. Another trend is called secularism, or worldliness. People seem to become less deeply religious, or separate religion from the practice of everyday life. Some, in an utterly un-Pancasilaist mood, even consider separating religion from the state! Another innate trait, this time to be criticized because all are equal in dignity and value, is the elitism of the lucky few. Earlier, we observed neofeudalistic tendencies, also called Mataramisasi, among the wealthy and powerful. These people apparently feel themselves to be much better than the rest, and they demonstrate it. Hence elitism. Somewhere in the course, it is suggested that the gap between rich and poor, alongside elitist, or priyayi-like, or exclusivistic, tendencies may give rise to jealousy; it could even cause a social storm. This is as close as we shall ever get to class analysis, as also hinted at by the last of the SARA spooks: *antar-golongan* (friction 'between groups').

Other, apparently indigenous problems inherent in modern Indonesian society have also been mentioned, such as dependency on government, nonparticipation in development programmes, pessimism, fatalism, and the absence of social responsibility. Why? Do people have reasons for such attitudes? We are not told — but isn't it strange that they are persistently present? The government is good and caring. How come some people have so little trust in its benevolence? The students may scrutinize experiences, and listen to the — quite audible — underground debates. The course merely bemoans these attitudes; they are undesirable. Then there are people who bribe, who are corrupt, who disregard the law, who are irresponsible, and who often enjoy powerful protection. Who they are, we are not told, and where such behaviour hails from is wrapped in mystery. Apparently, such behaviour is not uncommon. Is it related to 'feudalism'? Is it un-Indonesian behaviour, or is it as deeply rooted as the putative national personality?

The weapon needed to fight problems and undesirable traits is the Pancasila. Yet, I am not convinced that this leads to any result at all. I think the model of society that underlies the teachings is not only far behind the times, but possibly never had any validity. As far as there is a model, it is the one of the idealized community, or smaller still, of the family. That model is applied to wider society. Personal relationships are used to explain abstract and anonymous bonds. Inherent conflict should be compromised, not squarely faced. The most normal condition of society — opposed interests, opinions and values — is negated, and nothing more has been suggested than to be nice and polite to each other; to agree, and to reach unanimity. In the moral scheme of things, abstract society, and its inherent qualities, disappear, and remain beyond repair. No amount of values education can redress this. In the moral scheme, real problems — structurally rooted — remain unaddressable.

The implicit denial of the real state of affairs, and thus the refusal to analyse it in terms that befit it, leads to mendacity and hypocrisy. The students are aware of this. Pancasila education merely turns them into cynics. More tragic still, the type of moral education they are subjected to does not offer any guidelines for behaving morally and realistically in modern society. There, the autonomous conscience should be the compass to sail on. Everything in Pancasila education goes against this: autonomous individuals are dangerous to harmony. Indonesian individuals are part of the collectivity — they realize themselves in collectivism. Is there anything in Indonesia, apart from these palace-centred ideas, that ordains this? Let us reflect on this during our next excursion.

Fiction

I think that nobody really knows what collectivism is, though much of the mysterious East is thought to be characterized by it. Contemporary Eastern ideologues, propagating what they call Asian Values, are fond of invoking the spirit of familism, which they then extend far beyond the confines of any family, nuclear or extended, to encompass communities and other collectivities, until it covers the nation — which, in its turn, they easily equate with the state, and thus the incumbent regime. If there is any truth in 'collectivism', I think we should not extend it beyond the family — and even then ... .

Be this as it may, the orientalizing myth of collectivism — probably evoked in contrast to 'western' individualism — stands in need of debunking, and is easy to reject in the case of Java. As with most of the people living along the inner littoral of Southeast Asia, the Javanese reckon their descent bilaterally, meaning that female and male lines are equally important. They know no castes or clans, and ancestors beyond grandparents are rarely known. The focus of family life centres on the nuclear family or, if you want, is with the parents and their offspring. All this is very similar to what we find in most of the western world as well.

At the death of parents, inheritance is — normally — equally divided among the siblings and — economically, at least — everybody goes their own way. In other words, the brothers and sisters do not constitute a corporate group. They own their prime loyalty to their own nuclear families. This is not to say that they will not extend some help to needy relatives, or that they will not share certain burdens, but such assistance is essentially voluntary. If there is a measure of unity, then that is ritually expressed when the descendants of a couple congregate to celebrate *Lebaran* (New Year), or when they take care of parental graves.

There is no denying that extended family networks — say, aunts and uncles, cousins, nieces and nephews — often assume a certain importance. Within these, people belong loosely together, on a voluntary basis, and it is private individuals, not groups, that animate these webs of relatedness. In other words, the activation of family networks depends on individual persons who cultivate their own specific bonds with certain preferred family members — each and everybody in a group of siblings may thus see extended family relationships in his or her own way: such bonds are individual-centred.

This praxis of life indicates the real 'values'. There is little in living family relationships that is even vaguely reminiscent of collectivism. Sometimes, when whole villages were compelled to 'cooperate' to meet certain production quota — under the Cultivation System, or in the name of Development — the impression was made they were collectives. This comfortable administrative point of view was certainly not shared by the individuals concerned, although they also knew that fighting superior might would be self-defeating. We noted that the collectivity assumed a certain value in court and priyayi circles. Comfortable for the court were *kawula-Gusti* assumptions concerning the unity of rulers and ruled. Its executives, the priyayi, were indoctrinated to fuse with and realize themselves through service to the court — a doctrine still fully alive among the bosses of the army and the civil service corps, and further elaborated for the Ibu-ibu, the Mothers, of the Dharma Pertiwi and Dharma Wanita. Yet, compulsion does not make for spontaneous acceptance, and does not bring collectivism to life. It even stimulated the popularity of kebatinan as a way to self-realization. Kebatinan individualizes, it makes the self important.

The point of this excursion is to illustrate this by drawing from another source, namely, Javanese-authored literature. With the exception of a few authors, primarily Pramoedya Ananta Toer, Y.B. Mangunwijaya and, in his recent work, Umar Kayam, Javanese authors are not very informative about the society in which they situate their characters. Their writings tend to be individual-centred — often to the extreme. Their protagonists' relationships to their social environment remain vague; they are not socially situated, but live in worlds all their own. To demonstrate this, let me briefly review a few 'mystical' writings.

When Danarto published his prize winning story 'Rintrik' (1968), it was hailed as an important innovative 'trend' in short story writing that shared some characteristics with the absurdist novels of the Batak Iwan

Simatupang, for instance *Pilgrimage* (*Ziarah*, 1975). It became a movement, with Danarto's collection *Godlob* (1974), Kuntowijoyo's *Sermon on the Mount* (*Khotbah di atas Bukit*, 1976), and Harijadi S. Hartowardojo's *Date with Death* (*Perjandian dengan Maut*, 1976) as outstanding early examples.

These writings deal with intensely personal experiences set within the weird sceneries of mystical fantasizing. Their direction is away from social life, and turned inwards to mystical experience, the quest for death and detachment from life, with a strong emphasis on determinism and fate. Kuntowijoyo's *Sermon on the Mount* is characteristic of this genre. The author, a practising Muslim, told me he wrote his novel at a time when he was very disappointed with developments in Indonesia. Under the New Order, the hoped-for democratic, just, and prosperous society had become as utopian and beyond reach as under the previous regime.

The main character of the novel is Barman, a former diplomat and man of the world. When he retires to a provincial town, he soon finds his life intolerably dull. His son arranges a solution, finding him a villa on the slopes of a mountain, together with a beautiful, devoted, and relatively young mistress (Popi). The evening of his life thus promises to become a paradise.

One morning in his garden, he briefly meets a strange man who is not particularly respectful. Without introducing himself, the trespasser bluntly asks, 'What is your work?' and when Barman asks in return who he is, the stranger answers that he is 'the guardian of the mountain'. Later on they meet again — his name is Humam; he lives in a house a little above Barman's. During their walks, Humam talks in riddles. 'Our relationship is no relationship'; 'Don't worry about me; I have already let go the burden of life'; 'My being is my non-being, or the opposite'. He also gives mysterious answers, as in the following dialogue:

'What is your purpose?'
'There is no purpose; I merely am, the greatest joy'.
'And when we die?'
'Well, then we do not move any more'.
'Aren't you afraid?'
'Of all things, that is just what does not make me afraid at all'.

Initial attraction to Humam gradually becomes fascination with this strange recluse, who seems to know a secret and is not afraid of death. Little by little, Barman detaches himself from Popi, her good care, his house, and the enjoyment of the beauty of nature. When Humam dies, Barman moves into the former's house where he lives alone, cutting all links with his old way of life. His solitary existence, however, arouses the interest of nearby villagers: they have discovered a guru, a man who knows the secret, and after a while people come crowding into his yard day and night.

Barman knows that he knows nothing and has nothing to say. When he tries to flee from the crowd, he is stopped. 'Don't leave us, Father! Please speak to us. We are afraid. We suffer. We are confused'. When Barman finally speaks, he says only: 'We shall go to the top of the mountain'. In long procession, they start moving, Barman riding a horse. Upon their reaching the top, night falls, it gets cold, and the crowd grows restless. 'We want happiness! Do show us the way!' Suddenly, Barman has disappeared, and when his body is eventually found, they bury it on the very peak of the mountain. He did not speak; he was detached and vanished into the void.

More adventurous is Harijadi's story of Wardjo in his *Date with Death*. Wardjo's escape from the Japanese toward the end of their occupation of Indonesia sets him on a lonely journey through the mountains in which he is given the staff of invulnerability. Upon reaching the coast, he meets up with Nyai Loro Kidul, the mystical Queen of the Southern Ocean. He is overwhelmed by her beauty and personality; she warns him not to say foolish things or to promise anything. She tells him that she will make him her hero, a liberator of the people. In spite of her warnings, he promises to be faithful to her.

In the subsequent revolutionary struggle against the Dutch, he becomes a most successful commander, guided by inspiration from the Nyai. Upon meeting a girl, he falls in love, and guidance from the mystical queen becomes erratic. At a certain point, he decides he wants to marry his new love, despite the opposition of their respective parents. On their honeymoon, he is killed by Indonesian bullets during the APRA incident in Bandung. He deviated from his course, and instead of retiring into his mystical 'marriage', he became just another corpse, his attachment to life spelling his death.

The characteristic themes of the mystical novel, such as the individual quest for origin-and-destination; detachment from social attachments; the pull of death, are by no means restricted to this genre. These themes are so pervasive as to show up in one form or another in all kinds of Javanese fiction, the popular 'pop' novel being no exception. In *Vaingloriousness* (*Sok Nyentrik*, 1977), Eddy D. Iskandar introduces a family of humble origin, and their daughter Ichik. Upon winning the lottery, the family moves to Jakarta, where the rustic Ichik soon becomes the fashionable and extravagant Inge. After enjoying all the adventures a secondary school girl can have, she is finally overwhelmed by her own ostentatiousness, and feels increasingly confused. When she falls ill, she returns to the Sundanese village of her origin, back to her grandmother and former peasant boyfriend; she becomes Ichik again. In this way, she finds peace, and dies.

Moh. Diponegoro's *Cycle* (*Siklus*, 1975) is a kind of a 'pop' novel for grown-ups. It dwells on such matters as purpose, death and inevitability. Men are but puppets in the hands of fate, and what they may perceive as coincidence and mystery is really the expression of a divine plan that forces people to move on, whether they want to believe in predestination or not.

Individual-centredness is not necessarily mystically expressed, and many authors focus on individual loneliness per se. People are lonely because they fail to relate meaningfully to others; because of the dictates of fate; because of the failure to live up to traditional expectations; because they are powerless and poor in a big corrupt world that conceitedly pretends to be the bastion of righteousness and honourable tradition. It is of interest to note that protestations against the compulsion of tradition have been much more often elaborated by non-Javanese Indonesian authors, such as the Batak Armijn Pané in *Fetters* (*Belenggu*, 1940), the Sundanese Achdiat K. Mihardja in *The Atheist* (*Atheis*, 1949), and the Balinese Putu Wijaya in *Telegram* (1973). Javanese somehow seem to know that life is a lonely affair, and are apparently more inclined to accept things as they come. At the hands of gifted authors, such as Pramoedya and Subagio Sastrowardojo, existential loneliness has been most penetratingly described.

Pramoedya's early vision of life is most saliently recorded in his novelette *Life is not a Pleasant Party* (*Bukan Pasar Malam*, 1951). In it, he describes his visit to his dying father and family in Blora, after his detention by the Dutch, and subsequent struggles for survival in Jakarta. Everybody appears to be alone, subject to personal suffering, and incapable of relating in a meaningful fashion to others. 'In life we all come alone and die alone. Life should be a pleasant party where we come and go together'. Life, however, is not a pleasant happening, husband remaining stranger to wife; children growing up alien to their parents; brothers and sisters relating only vaguely to each other. People appear to be the victims of a life beyond their control.

These themes recur in his *Stories from Jakarta* (*Tjerita dari Jakarta*, 1957). The stories deal with the lives of the poor and suffering rejects of society. The revolution has run its course; what remains is disappointment, meaninglessness, disorientation. The vision of the early Pramoedya is basically critical of life itself, and not really addressed to social conditions. People are powerless and born losers; they are loners, outsiders to each other, mere observers. For the poor, the price of belonging is too high. Everybody needs to fend for himself: 'In our neighbourhood, poverty killed all ideals'.

In Subagio's collection *He-manship at Sumbing* (*Kedjantanan di Sumbing*, 1965), prowess and will to live are intimately related with death. All his characters are forced to fall back on themselves in their confrontation with life, where the other person is always just — or entirely — beyond reach. This lonely quest motivated the poet Rendra to give his only collection of prose writing the programmatic title *The Young Roamer* (*Dia sudah Bertualang*, 1963), reflecting his conviction that everybody has to seek his own solution to the riddle of life.

Loneliness within tradition, and the consciousness that to live is to fulfil fate, have been enlarged on in Umar Kayam's female characters, Bawuk and Sri Sumarah. These two novelettes, that were combined under the title *Sri Sumarah dan Bawuk* (1975), depict two apparently contradictory female characters who both follow the dictates of fate. Bawuk is somewhat obstinate in going her own way. As the daughter of a high-class family, she gets involved in a misalliance, eloping with a hard-headed fellow who becomes a communist leader. During the terror of 1965, she comes back to see her anxious relatives, only to leave them again in order to rejoin her husband in his hopeless struggle. Her decision and dedication are respected and respectable. She follows her fate to its ultimate consequences, surrendering herself, equating her being with the fate of her husband.

Sri Sumarah is a different character, entirely within the confines of tradition. From her earliest days, she has learned that a woman's life lies in devotion to her husband. She is nothing but mother and wife, and surrenders *(sumarah)* herself gracefully to circumstances, husband, and 'God'. Through accepting life as it comes, while finding satisfaction in her subservient role, she performs the mystical practice of self-surrender in everyday life. These same themes have also been worked out by the poet Linus Suryadi AG in *Pariyem's Confession* (*Pengakuan Pariyem*, 1981).

Although the writing just referred to is not the most recent, its themes keep recurring in the Javanese-authored literature. Seno Gumira Ajidarma's *Jazz, Perfume and the Incident* (*Jazz, Parfum dan Insiden*, 1996) provides us with a fine example. With it, we are presented with an ego-centred tale in which the ever-present ego figure remains nameless and vague. He 'is there', fantasizing, day-dreaming, commenting on women and perfume; being carried away by music; meditating about the glow of the sunset; sometimes observing, then being bombarded by reports of incomprehensible violence and brutality. If the book does anything at all, it creates an atmosphere that is a social commentary in itself.

The book opens on a poem that acknowledges the fleeting nature of existence, which, despite the will never to surrender, will lead to the grief of having to submit to fate. The symbol of the transitory character of life is the setting of the sun, especially the glorious excess of goldens, oranges and reds illuminating the office towers, reflecting and playing through their walls of glass before it all disappears into the murkiness of the night. Life changes, is fleeting; parting is dying a little bit. Yet, the transition itself, the flow from extravaganza to morbidity is fascinating: every moment of it should be experienced and consciously enjoyed.

The sun is setting, splashing colour. The narrator lives it. His room on the twentieth floor of an office tower is cascaded by the light broken and reflected by the city high-rises of glass. Telephone. That voice. Line to a woman enjoying the twilight from her place on a twentieth floor. Where? Somewhere. Behind which glass panel? Fascinating anonymity. Fascinating fantasy. Down below, thousands of office people with their portable phones and neckties. Here the lonely office, yet connected with a woman out there, somewhere, watching the same sunset. She is dressed in a blazer, tight skirt, on high-heeled shoes. Her nails are red.

'Are you in a blazer?'
'No, I took it off'
'Then, what's your blouse?'
'A "You-Can-See"'
'Wow'
'What's "wow"?'
'That shows your armpits'
'Well, if I lift my arms'
'Do you have hair under your arms?'

She is not in a tight-fitting skirt; she wears jeans. She has on jogging shoes. She does not make up her nails. Life is mere imagination. It's illusory. The telephone rings ... exactly on the dot.

Most often, episodes are narrated from this cubicle of glass on a twentieth floor. Telephones, pagers, documents, the walkman, they connect with or reach out into an essentially urban world. Is he a journalist? A writer? Why is he there at night, always at night, reading reports about 'The Incident', listening to jazz, fantasizing about women and perfume? Then, as a bomb-outrage: Timor 1991. November. Eight times the reader is confronted with the unspeakable atrocities, the sadism and systematic terror, the torture and lawlessness, the rape of a nation, and the rule of brutality unleashed by an army of occupation free from the reins of civilization. It is eyewitness reports; the commentary of a military commander — who defends his men; a governor who has the courage to side with the people.

Jazz. Jazz is life; it is wandering, exploring paths that go on and on, the music carrying the roamer. It fully fills existence; it enables one to be contented in solitude; it animates life; it is pure imagination. And so is perfume, the scent that gives individuality, a whiff of identity to women. Women drink with the narrator, are in clubs, on luxurious cruises, have sex, and provide for endless reverie. They walk into one's life, then disappear again, because 'We are finished'; 'We have nothing to say to each other'; 'We have no future'.

Relations with women reveal their unsatisfactoriness, and the fascination with departure. Things must end. We should be torn apart from each other. What is that strange drive of women — and very elegant and desirable ones at that — to love and be faithful to husbands who merely betray them? And yet, how is it possible that similar women, who experience their married lives as mere duty, can play around and enjoy their promiscuity? Is it any better among gays and lesbians? Relationships are treasonous; love is exploitative; still, people seek it because they often feel powerless in their wrestling match with solitude. And thus the I-figure relates to others, but only vaguely: to semi-tipsy ladies of the night; to willful women seeking the fleeting fun of sex; to unnamed others at the far end of a telephone line, then gladly abandoning them all to be absorbed by jazz.

Much of the book sounds the praises of anonymous urbanity, of losing oneself in music, perfume, and drink. Yet, can one lose oneself in the eyewitness reports about 'The Incident', about the unspeakable? 'But I cannot sleep, and in my dreams I see the army shooting people, spraying them with bullets, slaughtering them, and beating them up. Scattered bodies who still breathe, who ask for help, are merely run through with bayonets: all must die'. Then, still, it does not stop. 'I slept for two years', but the incident lives on, cruelty reproduces cruelty; bloodthirstiness is addictive; terror perpetuates itself. It is the most eloquent expression of a dehumanized authority intruding into the lives of ordinary people. It is a reign of arbitrariness and lies, of arrogance and denial that may confront its subjects at any moment, such as when the office is ransacked by a party of people in uniform.

'We know that you know. You know what we are here for. Better tell at once where you keep it'. [Drawers are turned over; files emptied on the floor; panels taken from the walls] 'We are looking for proof of subversion' ... 'You have contact with foreign NGOs that are antigovernment'.

'But they are merely helping with flood problems'.

'That means that they insult the government. As if we do not have food ourselves'.

'But their aid has nothing to do with food, but with a drainage system'.

'Doesn't matter; now we search'.

The captain of the party obviously stands for the paranoia, the systematic mistrustfulness of the authorities, and for disdain of people. When the office is in complete disarray, he still asks for understanding.

> 'Consider my staff. When they have a special operation, there is a special reward for them too. Nice to indulge themselves. Yet, God help you when, occasionally, we get carried away by our emotions. How is it possible not to get resentful these days when confronted with the extravagance, at the same time that we, who run the risk of being finished off by criminals, receive so little money. This is not just, is it? Think about it, is this justice?'
> ... Justice. A very intricate problem indeed.
> 'We, for instance, do know who the big-time criminals are in this city. Yet, what to do? They have strong backing. It's a real mafia. Many of the mysterious killings are never solved, are they? You too know what the situation is!'

This elicits a few reflections on the press in Indonesia. It is impossible to be honest. Writing, telling truth is a dangerous occupation, is endangering oneself. Thank God, the world is bigger than politics; we can write about sport and pop stars. Yet, even then. It does not take much for the authorities to muzzle critics or clamp down on the press. We have to accept the lies broadcast on television and by radio; we have to put up with the fabrications of the press. We are confronted with so much untruth that we cannot distinguish between falsehood and integrity any longer. Think about the 27 July 1996 affair. The only right choice to make is to lie.

Thus, go your own way as far as you can. Enjoy life. Escape from society — listen to your inner voice, to jazz; get carried away by perfume; enjoy the brilliance of sunset. Yet, how to deny The Incident? How to steer clear of life's basic unsatisfactoriness? Even urban anonymity is no guarantee for undisturbedness.

Summary

Most Javanese authors who write in Indonesian are given to describing individual-centred experience against the background of an amorphous but cruel society that it is beyond human volition or any hope of changing. Their descriptions of it remain vague, and often contrast with their elaboration of natural setting. Their characters travel through time rather than through social space, often having recourse to religion, mystical experience, or resignation to fate.

These authors tend to focus on the individual predicament, their characters relating to themselves rather than to their fellow men. Most often, they write about individuals who turn inward, exploring their own course irrespective of others or the society they live in. Theirs are novels of personal suffering, in which individuals have to find their own solutions. While lacking in social characterization beyond the relationships with near others, the Javanese Indonesian novel emphasizes the possibility of living with oneself, reflecting the powerful kebatinan tradition in Javanese culture. This is also exemplified by Rendra's credo:

Kemarin dan esok	Yesterday and to-morrow
adalah hari ini	occur to-day
Bencana dan keberuntungan	Catastrophe and good luck
sama saja	are the same
Langit diluar	Heaven outside
langit di badan	heaven inside
bersatu dalam jiwa	are united in the soul

Individual-centredness notwithstanding, characters remain psychologically unconvincing; their motivations remain as hazy as the social settings in which they are placed. Overall, the depictions are as 'flat' as shadow play puppets, allowing for little or no depth of the character, their actions seemingly being guided by fate and inevitability. In the novels concerned, individuals appear to stand apart from society; they do not appear to play an integral part. The authors are preoccupied with individual experience. Sometimes, they explain self-centred choices as reactions against the strong pressures to conform in ordinary social life. They do this through revealing society's hypocrisy and shortcomings; these impel the individual to go his own way. By writing such stories, these authors dissipate the myths of social harmony and collectivism that constitute 'official' Javanese reality.

CHAPTER 9

Summarizing patterns of thought

Order and leadership

The Javanese preoccupation with the ideals of unity and order —
which often appear to mean the same thing — may be interpreted as
the desire to escape from pluriformity and confusion. Unity and order
mean peacefulness, quiet continuity, mastery, success and well-being —
in brief, a moral and civilized way of life. It is threatened by nondomes-
ticated nature; untamed drives and personal desires; the lure of the spirit world, and life in modern urban anonymity.

While it is wise to do everything possible to maintain order and
guarantee continuity, for all that, turbulent currents may be flowing
beneath the calm surface. On occasion, encounters with disorder are
unavoidable. There are historical periods when, however much people
might like to distance themselves from it, they are inexorably caught up
in strife. In such periods it seems as if the king, the leader, has lost his
wahyu, his divine mandate to rule. This results in 'crazy times' when
people are guided by their passions and greed, by unbridled desire and
egoistic motives. From a modern point of view, it is a time of labour
unrest and strikes, of fierce political competition, of protest demonstra-
tions, of civil war and atrocities, of religious antagonism and glaring
social cleavages.

To be an effective leader, one must, naturally, overcome such
social turmoil. Even so, one's effectiveness is primarily an inner
resource. It is a matter of concentrating potency through overcoming
the turmoil within oneself. As a result, the accomplished practice of
kebatinan and efficacious leadership belong together. Through training
their inner resources, ideal leaders aim at overcoming their passions,
sensual desires and egoistic motives, taming their nature, as it were,
while generating discipline, insight, endurance, steadfastness, and inner
quiet. Imperturbable, they demonstrate the power of their batin and the
subtlety of their rasa, or sixth sense, by mastering and anticipating

events. Apparently attuned to the great scheme of necessity, kodrat, they naturally attract disciples and followers.

This is the picture the president projects of himself in his autobiography. His *Orde Baru* is a historical necessity on Indonesia's road to perfection, and this order revolves around his person; his concentrated potency inspires it. He is, therefore, not indebted to anybody. The other prominent architects of the New Order were merely attracted by the power of his batin; they are no more than henchmen and followers. The single person who needs positive recognition is thus his legitimator and predecessor, Sukarno. In this way, Soeharto can project himself as a kind of shadow crown prince, a secretive and necessary coordinate moving through Indonesian events until Supersemar, as the great kebeneran, draws him out on to the centre stage of history. From then onward, through the effective pacification of society, through the smothering of all protest and dissent, and through imposing order, security and stability, the president proves that he holds the wahyu, the divine mandate that legitimizes his rule more than do parliaments, elections exercises and suchlike.

Obligation

Sense of duty should be at the heart of everybody's life; it is not merely a matter of inferiors relating to superiors. Thus, parents have obligations toward their children; they must rear and protect, teach, and worry about them. Such is their task. They must prepare their offspring for life, see to it that they grow up human and respectable, conscious of self and others. They are supposed to arm their charges with a good example and right teaching. Despite good intentions, educating children remains a precarious endeavour. For this reason, many parents take recourse to the practice of austerities, minor forms of asceticism, slametan rituals, and sacrifices. This expresses their earnest solicitude, or prihatin, and the hope of invoking salutary continuity.

In all this, the child appears to be on the receiving end, as the one who benefits from nurture and care, attention and teaching. This lays the basis of one of the most important attributes of personhood, namely, the sense of gratitude, obligation, dependence and identity.

Alone, nobody can survive; as social beings, people depend on each other, first of all on morally superior parents. This in turn gives rise to obligations of respect, submission, and recognition of sacrifice, and thus of gratitude. In a general sense, to be in the care of somebody places the recipient under an *utang budi* (moral obligation), that is a debt of gratitude. Not to acknowledge this debt is more than despicable; it is to be morally defective.

This sense of obligation to others is most pertinent to Javanese existence; it is its moral touchstone, and cements relationships. As a theme, it surfaces all the time in Pancasila moral education, in which obligation is explained to root in dependence. Thus, by implication, it censures those who are so presumptuous and arrogant as to think that they did it all alone, that they achieved their success independently, that they are 'self-made men'. Such 'individualism' verges on culpable self-glorification. It equates with not knowing gratitude, with negating one's essential humanity, with losing one's Javanese personhood. When people comment that certain public figures 'have lost their Javanese qualities', they mean that such persons must be considered to be beyond the pale of civilized life, since exalted position has blinded them to obligation and morality; they have opted out of the moral order.

Religious preoccupations

The position of parents is quasi-religious. As elders, they are closer to the Origin, to the sources of identity and wisdom, to Life, the line of which they must continue by procreating and rearing children. The fulfilment of this task makes them worthy of the highest respect, and justifies the 'cult of parents'; parents themselves become *pepundhèn* (objects of veneration). The religious dimension of this 'cult' becomes clearer still from the dependence of children on their elders' blessing. Even when already well established and financially independent, at least once a year at Lebaran, siblings should gather at the ancestral home to ask for parental forgiveness and favour. This dependency continues when parents have passed away, because children are expected to visit their graves to make offerings and seek the beneficence they need for a peaceful existence.

An interesting aspect of the parent-child relationship is that it locates certain 'religious' elements squarely in this world. Children must pay homage to parents; depend upon their blessing; commit sin against them — obstinacy and insolence against parents not only invoking walat (supernatural retaliation), but also causing concrete feelings of guilt. Altogether, it is safe to say that the bond between parents and children provides the solid ground for the idea of moral hierarchy.

This idea easily enlarges to the perception of society as a moral construct. Respect for social order becomes a person's foremost obligation. Good community relations transcend individual interests. This striving is also expressed in the core ritual of the slametan, which seeks the blessing of ancestors and souls for slamet, for quiet and peaceful continuity. It demonstrates the nearness and accessibility of supernature and the desire to live in harmony with its beneficial forces. Some of these forces are located at graves, especially those of mystically inspired religious teachers and kings; such places become pepundhèn or *kramatan*, sacred spots where the faithful seek inspiration, potency, or lottery numbers. To be successful in such quests, adepts normally practise some form of asceticism, or sacrifice, at those places. On the other hand, in order to ward off inauspiciousness, ritual may be needed to avoid or reverse bad constellations, and offerings may be brought to appease or cajole invisible, yet near, spiritual beings.

It is clearly impossible to analyse these ideas in terms of sacred and profane, as is sometimes done in western sociology. Javanese thinking emphasizes the oneness of life, in which cosmic conditions are reflected by life on earth, and in which supernatural events penetrate everyday experiences. Supernature is inhabited by all kinds of spiritual beings, whose intentions and potential may be beneficial or disruptive, but, so much is certain, whose powers affect those in the visible realm. People are therefore preoccupied with the acquisition of blessing from those who can protect, and with increasing personal efficacy. In brief, religious practice is a relationship with power that is future-directed, not so much toward an afterlife, but as an activity seeking auspiciousness in the here-and-now. This quality is also exemplified by the practice of kebatinan for the sake of generating potency and efficacy.

Be this as it may, kebatinan reveals essential traits of a philosophy of life and the shaping of culture. Religious practice and mystical kebatinan are parts of kejawèn culture, and although the religious element is not necessarily dominant, neither can it be eliminated from a style of conceptualization that emphasizes wholeness and the unity of Life. In the Pancasila, the nature of this unity is referred to as Ketuhanan, the Divine, which may either be thought of as a transcendent God or an encompassing All-Soul. This latter, less personal, notion allows for equating the Divine with Life, or with Necessity, with kebatinan becoming the endeavour — quasi-secular, quasi-religious — to be attuned to that which is greater than man, and to feel this in one's inner being.

We have noted that this exercise aims at developing a strong batin (character) and a refined, accomplished rasa — personal attributes that underscore individuality, subjectivism, and that proclaim the validity of individual experience and personal feeling as the ultimate touchstones for truth. This stands in opposition to the pressure to conform with expectations and wishes of the powers-that-be; it generates a general distaste for religious dogmatism, and a fascination with mystery and esoteric affairs. Religious life, therefore, is felt to be a private affair. This does not negate the usefulness of regular religious practice, of following the rules of the faith, or of seeking God in Mecca, but people who want to go another way should be free to do so, religious practice being an open-ended quest for safety, efficacy, blessing, and personal fulfilment.

Syncretism?

The recognition that people should be autonomous in their relationships with the spiritual results in a multitude of mystical theories and practices that, however much their similarities, are always claimed to be the personal revelations of each guru and individual virtuoso. In this climate, one can imagine that there is a general distaste for religious dogma, proclaimed orthodoxy, or systematic theology; it is individual visionary encounters that are held to reveal experiential, direct truth.

This general stance allows for incorporation of all kinds of elements from other discourses that have come to the attention of the adepts. Some generously mix in Muslim ideas with the Hindu-Buddhist heritage from the period preceding the advent of Islam; others juxtapose Catholicism, ancestor worship and theosophy; others still relish combining cabalism, freemasonry and Javanese concepts of biology, without ever bothering for a moment about questions of compatibility. This licence is often labelled syncretism.

I am not convinced that this term explains what is going on; it merely establishes the fact of mixing, but does not delve into the cultural constellation in which the blending takes place, and so it is not descriptive of causes or the field of action. Personal speculation may be seen as a generic trait of Javanese religious thinking. After all, religion is concerned with the unseen and mysterious, and its location is more within the person than in social life. Syncretism, then, is merely a logical outcome of these basic conditions.

In the kejawèn frame of mind, rationality always combines with intuition, it is rasa-thinking grounded in the recognition that there is always something nonexplicit and irrational within almost every phenomenon and experience. This also inspires the sense of distrust towards western science and linear rationality. Some Javanese are very ready to point out that, for them, the way the sciences claim to progress at once shows up their basic flaw. Science, in its search for true statements, reasons deductively from premises that, at the same time, it attempts to disprove and reject, nothing apparently having any permanent status — and so, what can be the value of the 'truth' arrived at?

Javanese reasoning, in contrast, is more inductive, analyzing experience and necessity while grasping the essence, the *rasa* of phenomena intuitively, that is to say directly, without tortuous theoretical constructions and tedious research. Perhaps this is one reason, too, why science fails to flourish in Indonesia and why there is little indigenous cultural input as far as the social branches are concerned. As part of prestigious modernity, and in response to the demand for education, the western sciences are taught as systems of terms, concepts and rules that are taken straight from foreign-written textbooks. When translated into research, formal procedures, that appear to have worked themselves free from any theoretical coherence, are applied to particular phenomena, yielding single statements about, for instance, the ethos of work of factory labour, or the noninnovativeness of native entrepreneurship, without considering starvation wages, or access to credit.

While there are many other reasons for the uninspired intellectual life at many a university, two factors may well contribute to the failure of indigenous higher education in making a meaningful contribution to shaping modern life so far. The first is a general approach to knowledge that surfaces clearly in the religious mentality that takes pleasure in mystical speculation, and the second the relative rigidity of social life that suppresses creativity. Yet, most people are unfazed by such critical observations, because the scientific enterprise has been cut loose from its western moorings; it became embedded in a syncretizing, or rather synthetizing environment, in which there is little awareness that the path science follows is logical and analytical, rather than constructive and compounding.

Thanks to generous infusions of all kinds of uncritical assumptions and undigested theories from western universities, discussions in Indonesia remain extremely blurred and irrelevant:

> The country is on its way to the Pancasila society. It will take off and become an industrial nation; it will be steeped in a culture of science and technology; this will produce a new type of man who is innovative, democratic and meritocratic. To reach this, a new cultural strategy is needed that is functional, integrative, and aimed at building a new ethos of work with international standards. This will overcome the collectivist characteristic of the village; this latter trait still leads to amoral familism which is the source of clanism, ethnicism, and groupism (Sularto 1990:54-6).

The above is not presented as balderdash. This type of jumble of concepts occurs not infrequently in serious discussions among people, many of them holding degrees from reputable universities, who are deeply concerned about the course the nation is steering. Their deliberations come across as unrealistic; their assumptions as wild; their vision as fantastic. What they are doing is syncretizing; they are not analyzing the situation on the ground, they are not scrutinizing structure or looking for basic causes. The course of Indonesian society is given, its development inevitable, and people need to be prepared for it, and so textbooks are written about Pancasila economy, sociology and philosophy. The production of books, treatises, and mystifications about Pancasila — written by all sorts of academics — is so impressive that it probably runs second only to comparable religious and mystical writings. In this intellectual climate, nobody should be amazed if one university or another opens a department of Pancasilalogy in the years to come.

This delight in stirring all kinds of unconnected things together, of compounding them, is, on the one hand, related to rasa-thinking and, on the other, to the obsession with oneness. This drive toward unity always subsumes distinctions, striving upwards, away from facts and analytical hair-splitting. In that process, incompatibilities gradually disappear, and it is therefore different from just syncretizing. What it seeks to accomplish is synthesis, the quiet order of undifferentiated union.

Scientific versus moralistic thinking

According to one of Indonesia's own keenest social critics, the priest-author-architect Y.B. Mangunwijaya, Indonesian culture has not yet reached the stage of the Enlightenment. Thinking is still mythological, the individual still dominated by the group, and society by dynastic rule. Few and frustrated are the people who have grasped what western science is about, and who are adept at handling theory. Systematic, disciplined abstraction is hard to comprehend, and so truth remains derivable from experience and pleasant speculation.

It is still strange for most to distance themselves from personal practice; as a result, abstract ideas, such as the public interest or the rule of law, are extremely difficult to grasp. Society is still seen as it is lived, as ties to concretely known individuals, whose common good is phrased in terms of mutual claims and obligations, and whose just, or ethical, behaviour depends on their status so defined.

Equating persons with their status, power, or obligations, makes them very tangible, and sets them far apart from the abstracted 'generalized other'. Perhaps for no other reason than this one, the actualization of democracy becomes a nonprobability. It simply cannot be imagined. Needless to say, in such a situation political ideologies — being theoretical by their nature — cannot thrive, and the sociological imagination does not develop. Rather, society is perceived as an aggregate of individuals who cluster in families, and who need to be hierarchically controlled. Seen from this viewpoint, it is not poverty that is the problem, but the presence of many poor people. In this way, solutions to social problems are thought to be rooted in individual ethical behaviour. If people know their place and fulfil its inherent obligations, are faithful in living their religious duties, and strive to live according to the Pancasila, poverty and other problems will evaporate; social life will become exemplary, with Indonesia shining as a beacon for the world.

Problems originate from individual moral decay, and thus individuals need guidance, teaching, and leadership to keep them on the right track. They need to be constantly exhorted to discipline themselves; cooperate; make the election a success; devote themselves to society; plan their families; live according to the Pancasila, the Pancakarsa, the Panca Dharma Wanita, and so on.

These admonishments show more than just a delight in slogans and self-fulfilling mantras. They also demonstrate an approach to societal questions that is moral and intuitive. It is not a systematic theoretical approximation of reality, however often maxims are dressed up in modern gear. The overuse of terms, such as human rights; take-off; innovation; democracy; development; rule of law, only demonstrates that they have been freed from any context in which they make sense. The content of these dictums is no more than a moral appeal to help reach a destination that is, anyway, inevitable.

While the social sciences can develop only by drawing inferences from observed facts in their quest for theoretical development — and thus must devote a great deal of attention to actual circumstances and facts — and by producing merciless diagnostic assessments of the state of affairs, the moralistic approach is not so much interested in carefully dissecting the actual situation and its history. It is future-oriented, more interested in where we are heading than in where we are, while seeking direction more in inspiration than in the confrontation with obdurate facts.

Ethics

Oneness in the sense of unity means good order, smooth relationships, the absence of disturbance; it means harmony and conformity, a static state that is calm and pleasing. It is a sign of mastery. The contrary situation, disunity, means conflict and strife, opposition and unruliness. It is mastery lost, unpleasant, exciting and wild. It is graceless.

Things should be presented in fine order, be accomplished gracefully and elegantly executed. Such smoothness, such refinement, such elegance, or grace is *alus*. It is culture at its best. And so it is alus to demonstrate mastery of the Javanese speech levels, to be aware of self and others, to have fine manners and a modest bearing. These are the marks of civilized persons, reflecting inner discipline and calm. Their accomplished self-presentation adorns the world, makes it a more beautiful, a better place. Such a person is good.

Alus contrasts with *kasar*, which is the absence of good manners, the stir of monkeys, the turmoil of emotions, the lack of education, the pretension of clowns, the threat of 'communists', the straightforwardness of criticism, the rebelliousness of disagreement, the openness of conflict, and the lack of diplomacy. Kasar is untamed, is closeness to nature; it is falling short of civilization.

The imposition of order is good in itself, because order is what should be. To impose order, power is needed, be it the power of self-discipline to achieve inner calm, or the power to make others follow and obey. The exercise of power can be alus, as in the image of the exemplary leader whose charisma commands spontaneous submission; or gross, such as firing into crowds of unarmed demonstrators.

This latter habit is quite widespread in Southeast Asia, massacres — whether at Mendiola or on the island of Negros; on Rajdamnoen or at Thammasat; in Dili, the Lampongs, or Tanjungpriok — apparently being a ready means to compel obedience, and the serene order of the cemetery.[7] The violence is warranted, because rebellious behaviour is

7 The cases referred to here are the Mendiola massacre at the presidential palace in Manila, February 1987; at Escalante on Negros, September 1985; at the Democracy Monument in Bangkok, May 1992; at Thammasat University there, October 1973 and 1976; in Dili, East Timor, November 1992; the Lampongs, South Sumatra, early 1989, and in the port district of Jakarta, September 1984.

disgraceful, is questioning the authority — the wahyu — of 'legitimate' government, is an offence and gross behaviour.

The end justifies the means, although it is better if the means are alus too. Mysterious murders, such as the so-called *petrus (penembakan misterius)* killings of petty criminals by covert, 'official' murder squads, are therefore far more acceptable; the eradication of a Sumbawan village was even so successful that it attracted almost no publicity at all. In this way, the kasar insult of disagreement did not lead to the injury of loss of alus face. Be this as it may, violent means are felt to be suitable for dealing with kasar people, who can only be reined in by force because this is the only thing they seem to understand.[8]

Command can be alus too, such as compelling hints or persuasive appeals that nobody will ignore or refuse. And if, in civil society, people still politely protest by signing a petition, by declaring themselves presidential candidates, or by voicing displeasing opinions while abroad, then alus means will be mobilized too. Perhaps their relatives will be dismissed from their jobs, or be refused access to the university; perhaps they find that they cannot open a bank account, or are found ineligible for credit; maybe they suddenly find that former associates are avoiding them, or that they cannot get a passport if they want to travel. Sometimes, when they are placed under house arrest *(di-rumah-sajakan)*, they are said to have been promoted to the status of *doktorandus, Drs.* (an academic title). In extreme cases they may enjoy the full hospitality of the state in prisons called *Lembaga Pemasyarakatan*, in fine, socialization institutions, that should, from their very name, prepare inmates for re-entry into society. Yet, some communists are apparently so incapable of rehabilitation that, despite twenty-five years of serious efforts on the side of the authorities, they are finally disposed of in front of a firing squad.

The more refined the better, both in the aesthetical and ethical senses. Order is not only a good, it is good as such. Good and beautiful belong together; to speak High Javanese is to speak good language, to

---

8 This attitude, which is shared with the outdated priyayi two-class perception of society, is still very widespread among educated and powerful people. They hold that measures aimed at the improvement of life — Family Planning, Development — should initially be forced upon the *wong cilik* (small people); later, when they understand the benefits, they will certainly be grateful.

obey one's parents is good behaviour, a sign of mature morality, and the less stir one causes, the more one is a graceful and moral man. Conflict is disgusting and distasteful; it must be eradicated to restore the stillness of unity that is, in itself, the sign of ethically accomplished life.

Bibliographic note

It has been our policy not to lard the main body of text with references and footnotes. Here is the place to redress these omissions and to give some information about the literature from which facts and inspiration have been drawn. Still, no attempt will be made to be complete; the titles to be discussed here, however, are authoritative guides to a fuller exposition of the subject matter; they contain references to less accessible literature, such as books in languages other than English, and unpublished academic dissertations.

Still, such dissertations provide the richest source on kebatinan mysticism. Since Clifford Geertz, in his monumental *The Religion of Java*, noticed the trend that mysticism might be spreading, the practice of kebatinan began to attract the attention of academic researchers and theologians. The latter began to publish vigorously in the late 1960s. Harun Hadiwijono's *The Concept of Man in the Present Javanese Mysticism* is an available example. Anthropological research began later — my own dissertation *Mysticism and Everyday Life in Contemporary Java* being an early instance. Less accessible are the studies by Paul Stange (Sumarah), P.P. Sitompul (Subud), Julia D. Howell and S.A. Patty (about Javanist thinking and practice in general), S. de Jong (Pangestu), Margo L. Lyon (Javanese Hinduism), and O.G. Howe (Sumarah).

Because the Subud movement gained many adherents in the western world, it really went international, meaning that it boasts of an abundance of documentation in English, comprising both the founding ideas, and the commentary and experiences of enthusiastic followers. All this, plus interesting reflections on mysticism and its Javanese variants, have been brought together by Antoon Geels in his *Subud and the Javanese Mystical Tradition*.

Reasons for the growth of mysticism in post-independence Indonesia have been advanced by most authors on the subject. Pertinent to the early period are Koentjaraningrat in his *Javanese Culture*, Geertz in *Religion*, and the Catholic priest Rahmat Subagyo. These reflections have been brought up to date by Paul Stange, whose many essays on mysticism and Java have been published in as many dif-

ferent journals and collections. Relevant to the recent history of kebatinan movements are his 'Religious Change in Contemporary Southeast
Asia', which is partly based on an earlier article '"Legitimate" Mysticism
in Indonesia', which must also be credited for succinctly presenting the
main teachings of four well-known mystical groups.

Geertz's *Religion* became probably best known for its still influential tripartite description of 'streams' of religious practice in Java. Ever
since he published his dissertation in 1960, the concepts of abangan,
santri, and priyayi have been used and discussed in the literature, to the
point that they even entered Indonesian schoolbooks. In despite of persistent attempts to the contrary, namely, to create a unitary Pancasila
state, the cleavage between politicized Islam versus the rest — a rift
first noted as the santri-abangan opposition — still seems to bedevil
Indonesia, although it would be far too simplistic to reduce this struggle
to 'religion'.

The interpretation of kejawèn culture as a colonial product has
been most convincingly argued by John Pemberton in his *On the Subject
of "Java"*. As we have seen, postindependence mysticism also hails from
the late colonial period, and its transplantation into the present seems
to influence the cultural construction of the New Order regime.
Pemberton draws our attention to comparable transplantations. These,
as 'recovered origins', are henceforward perpetuated in marriage ceremonies and other rituals that seem to evoke generic Indonesianness —
albeit in a "Javanese" guise. In a similar stereotypical manner, the New
Order's 'Beautiful Indonesia' in Miniature Theme Park is thought to
evoke authenticity by folklorizing and museumizing 'culture'. In a way,
the New Order presents itself as a cultural order, and cloaks its politics
in an idiom of presumed kejawèn tradition. The new kraton is in
Jakarta, and many people seem to agree. Authenticity false as the eye-
lashes of the daughter of the pope!

Laurie J. Sears also places Javanese culture outside the harness of
authenticity. In her *Shadows of Empire: Colonial Discourse and Javanese
Tales*, she argues for the contemporaneity of culture — instead of its
endurance and essential qualities — by demonstrating how the shadow
theatre mythology was affected in style and content by the ways and
fashions of imperial days. Be this as it is — and in spite of the use of
wayang to disseminate the messages of the day — there is plenty of lit-

erature emphasizing the essential Javaneseness contained in wayang, and its mystical messages. Of special interest is Mangkunegara VII's exposition on the secretive, deep nature of the mythology, which was composed in 1932, thus at the time that current aliran mysticism originated. For further interpretations of wayang — and disregarding a vast literature — I found Boediardjo, 'Wayang: a Reflection of the Aspirations of the Javanese', and the essentializing Ward Keeler in *Javanese Shadow Plays, Javanese Selves*, relevant.

The *Wédhatama* remains a short text basic to Javanist understanding of spiritual knowledge, practice, and mysticism. However abstruse specialists hold this didactic poem to be, the fine and clear translation by Stuart Robson reveals many patterns of thought characteristic of kebatinan mysticism. In this book we have retraced these patterns as they surface in the official textbooks on the state ideology. The history, development and current content of this ideology have been made available by Eka Darmaputera in his *Pancasila and the Search for Identity and Modernity in Indonesian Society*, and Douglas E. Ramage in his *Politics in Indonesia*. The first of these books presents us with a 'synthetic' Indonesian point of view that comes close to school-text wisdom, while the latter contains a western oriented analysis of 'the Pancasila discourse'.

A commendable historical background is provided by M.C. Ricklef's *A History of Modern Indonesia*. Adam Schwarz's, for official Indonesia controversial, *A Nation in Waiting: Indonesia in the 1990s* brings us up to date. Its foci are with politics, economics, Islam, and the 'great enigma': Indonesia after Soeharto. With history apparently always in the making, Javanese culture is in perpetual flux. With *Inside Indonesian Society: Cultural Change in Java*, I tried to chart the most important changes over the past twenty-five years. In *Inside Southeast Asia: Religion. Everyday Life. Cultural Change*, I reflected on Southeast Asian commonalities and cultural persistence in change. For all sorts of further anthropological references, up to the 1980s, Koentjaraningrat's *Javanese Culture* remains an indispensable, encyclopedic source.

References

Bahan Penataran P4. Jakarta: BP-7 Pusat, 1990.

Boediardjo, 'Wayang: a reflection of the aspirations of the Javanese'. H. Soebadio and C.A. du Marchie Sarvaas (eds), *Dynamics of Indonesian history*. Amsterdam, etc.: North-Holland Publishing Co., 1978.

Darmaputera, Eka, *Pancasila and the search for identity and modernity in Indonesian society: a cultural and ethical analysis*. Leiden, etc.: E.J. Brill, 1988.

Departemen Pendidikan dan Kebudayaan, *Pendidikan Pancasila dan kewarganegaraan*. (SLTP 3; SLTA 1, 2, 3). Jakarta: Balai Pustaka, 1996.

Geels, Antoon, *Subud and the Javanese mystical tradition*. Richmond, Surrey: Curzon Press, 1997.

Geertz, Clifford, *The religion of Java*. London: Collier-MacMillan, The Free Press of Glencoe, 1960.

Hadiwijono, Harun, *The concept of man in the present Javanese mysticism*. Baarn: Bosch en Keuning N.V., 1967.

Kartodirdjo, Sartono, *Protest movements in rural Java*. Singapore: Oxford University Press, 1973.

Keeler, Ward, *Javanese shadow plays, Javanese selves*. Princeton, N.J.: Princeton University Press, 1987.

Koentjaraningrat, *Javanese culture*. Singapore: Oxford University Press, 1985.

Mangkunegara VII of Surakarta, K.G.P.A.A., *On the wayang kulit (purwa) and its symbolic and mystical elements*. Ithaca: Cornell University, Southeast Asia Program, Data Paper no. 27, 1957.

Mulder, Niels, *Mysticism and everyday life in contemporary Java*. Singapore: Singapore University Press, 1980 (2nd. ed.).

Mulder, Niels, *Inside Indonesian society: cultural change in Java*. Amsterdam: The Pepin Press, 1996.

Mulder, Niels, *Inside Southeast Asia: religion – everyday life – cultural change*. Amsterdam: The Pepin Press, 1996.

Pemberton, John, *On the subject of "Java"*. Ithaca and London: Cornell University Press, 1994.

Ramage, Douglas E., *Politics in Indonesia: democracy, Islam and the ideology of tolerance*. London, New York: Routledge, 1995.

Ricklefs, Merle C., *A history of modern Indonesia, c. 1300 to the present*. London: The Macmillan Press, 1981.

Robson, Stuart, *The Wédhatama. An English translation*. Leiden: KITLV Press, 1990.

Schwarz, Adam, *A nation in waiting: Indonesia in the 1990s*. Boulder, San Francisco: Westview Press, 1994.

Sears, Laurie J., *Shadows of empire: colonial discourse and Javanese tales*. Durham, London: Duke University Press, 1996.

Soeharto, Ramadhan K.H., G. Dwipayana, *Soeharto: sebuah autobiografi*. Jakarta: P.T. Citra Lamtoro Gung Persada, 1989.

Soeharto, *Butir-butir budaya Jawa*. Jakarta: Yayasan Purna Bhakti Pertiwi, 1990.

Stange, Paul, '"Legitimate" mysticism in Indonesia'. *Review of Indonesian and Malayan Affairs*, vol. 20/2, 1986.

Stange, Paul, 'Religious change in contemporary Southeast Asia'. N. Tarling (ed), *The Cambridge History of Southeast Asia*, vol. 2. Cambridge: Cambridge University Press, 1992.

Subagyo, Rahmat, 'Kepercayaan — kebatinan, kerohanian, kejiwaan dan agama'. *Majalah Spektrum*, vol. 3, 1973.

Sularto, St. (ed), *Menuju masyarakat baru Indonesia*. Jakarta: Kompas/Gramedia, 1990.

Tim Sosiologi, *Panduan belajar sosiologi 2*. Jakarta: Yudhistira, 1996.

Index of names

Subject index

Glossary

abangan	nonpractising Muslim; syncretist
agama	religion
aliran	organized stream of thought
alus	refined; etheral
bandar	gambling intermediary; bank holder; croupier
batin	inner; spiritual; essential
belum	not yet (Indonesian)
BKKI	Badan Kongres Kebatinan Indonesia
BK51	Badan Kongres Kepercayaan Kejiwaan Kerohanian Kebatinan Indonesia
budaya	mind, intellect; culture, civilization
darma (dharma)	(preordained) task, obligation
dhukun	shaman; morally ambiguous mediator between nature and supernature
durung jawa	not yet Javanese
gotong-royong	mutual assistance
gusti	master, lord
hakékat	truth; essence. Third stage of mystical practice
Hyang Suksma	'God'; All Soul
Ibu	lit. Mother, hence Mrs. Because of the state, i.e. Dharma Wanita, explaining it as subservience, many modern women take their distance from this term
jiwa	soul; psyche
jumbuhing kawula lan Gusti	the blending of mystical servant/slave and Lord
kasar	gross
kasektèn	supernatural power; sacred potency
kasunyatan	Truth; truth in religious sense
kawula	slave, servant
kebatinan	science of inner man; mysticism; the practice of these
kebeneran	co-incidence; manifest truth
kejawèn	(concerning) the culture of the South-Central Javanese principalities

Ketuhanan	The Divine
kiai	adept (Muslim) teacher
klenik	(black) magical mysticism
kodrat	omnipotence; predestination
lair	outward; physical
laku	practice in accordance with mystical insight
latihan	(mystical) exercise
Lebaran	Javanese Muslim New Year
makripat	gnosis; intuitive knowledge of 'God'. Highest stage of mystical practice
mamayu hayuning buwono	to beautify/adorn the world
mufakat	unanimous agreement/decision (result of *musyawarah*)
musyawarah	mutual consultation (in order to reach *mufakat*)
ngèlmu	esoteric knowledge/science
olah rasa	training the *rasa*
Pakem	Pengawas Aliran Kepercayaan Masyarakat
pamrih	self-interest
persatuan dan kesatuan	unity and integrity
PNI	Partai Nasional Indonesia
prihatin	(practice/attitude of) solicitude
priyayi	(king's) official
pusaka	sacred/potent (protective) heirloom
ramé ing gawé	diligent
rasa	essence; intuitive inner feeling (sixth sense)
roh	spirit
RT	Rukun Tetangga
rukun	concord
samadi	(insight) meditation; meditation to increase potency
Sang Hyang	'God'
sangkan-paran	origin-and-destination
santri	practising Muslim
SARA	sensitive issues not to be publicly discussed
sepi ing pamrih	unselfish
slamet	well-being
slametan	communal religious meal

sujud	surrendering self to 'God'
Supersemar	the *kebeneran* inaugurating the New Order
tapa	austerities; ascetic exercises
tarékat	second stage of mystical practice. Muslim mystical brotherhood
ukum pinesthi	cosmic law; principle of necessity
ulema, ulama	scholar of Islam; Muslim religious teacher or leader
Urip	Life
wahyu	revelation; charisma; God's gift/blessing/mandate/ legitimation
Wawasan Nusantara	(the unitary) Archipelago Concept
wayang	shadow theatre
zaman édan	crazy times
zaman mas	golden times